POWERP
FOR WINDOWS
FOR
DUMMIES®

Quick Reference

by Camille McCue

**IDG
BOOKS**
WORLDWIDE

IDG Books Worldwide, Inc.
An International Data Group Company

Foster City, CA ✦ Chicago, IL ✦ Indianapolis, IN ✦ New York, NY

PowerPoint® 2000 For Windows® For Dummies® Quick Reference

Published by
IDG Books Worldwide, Inc.
An International Data Group Company
919 E. Hillsdale Blvd.
Suite 400
Foster City, CA 94404
www.idgbooks.com (IDG Books Worldwide Web site)
www.dummies.com (Dummies Press Web site)

Library of Congress Catalog Card No.: 98-88741

ISBN: 0-7645-0451-7

Printed in the United States of America

10 9 8 7 6 5 4 3 2 1

1P/SQ/QU/ZZ/IN

Distributed in the United States by IDG Books Worldwide, Inc.

Distributed by CDG Books Canada Inc. for Canada; by Transworld Publishers Limited in the United Kingdom; by IDG Norge Books for Norway; by IDG Sweden Books for Sweden; by Woodslane Pty. Ltd. for Australia; by Woodslane (NZ) Ltd. for New Zealand; by TransQuest Publishers Pte Ltd. for Singapore, Malaysia, Thailand, Indonesia, and Hong Kong; by ICG Muse, Inc. for Japan; by Norma Comunicaciones S.A. for Colombia; by Intersoft for South Africa; by Le Monde en Tique for France; by International Thomson Publishing for Germany, Austria and Switzerland; by Distribuidora Cuspide for Argentina; by Livraria Cultura for Brazil; by Ediciones ZETA S.C.R. Ltda. for Peru; by WS Computer Publishing Corporation, Inc., for the Philippines; by Contemporanea de Ediciones for Venezuela; by Express Computer Distributors for the Caribbean and West Indies; by Micronesia Media Distributor, Inc. for Micronesia; by Grupo Editorial Norma S.A. for Guatemala; by Chips Computadoras S.A. de C.V. for Mexico; by Editorial Norma de Panama S.A. for Panama; by American Bookshops for Finland. Authorized Sales Agent: Anthony Rudkin Associates for the Middle East and North Africa.

For general information on IDG Books Worldwide's books in the U.S., please call our Consumer Customer Service department at 800-762-2974. For reseller information, including discounts and premium sales, please call our Reseller Customer Service department at 800-434-3422.

For information on where to purchase IDG Books Worldwide's books outside the U.S., please contact our International Sales department at 317-596-5530 or fax 317-596-5692.

For consumer information on foreign language translations, please contact our Customer Service department at 1-800-434-3422, fax 317-596-5692, or e-mail rights@idgbooks.com.

For information on licensing foreign or domestic rights, please phone +1-650-655-3109.

For sales inquiries and special prices for bulk quantities, please contact our Sales department at 650-655-3200 or write to the address above.

For information on using IDG Books Worldwide's books in the classroom or for ordering examination copies, please contact our Educational Sales department at 800-434-2086 or fax 317-596-5499.

For press review copies, author interviews, or other publicity information, please contact our Public Relations department at 650-655-3000 or fax 650-655-3299.

For authorization to photocopy items for corporate, personal, or educational use, please contact Copyright Clearance Center, 222 Rosewood Drive, Danvers, MA 01923, or fax 978-750-4470.

About the Author

Camille McCue has used PowerPoint since its beginnings, watching it grow from an infant presentation tool into a killer application. She built her first slide shows — chock full of Newton's Laws and Far Side cartoons — while tele-teaching high school physics via satellite. (And like *all* science teachers, she worships Gary Larson!)

A bona fide Longhorn, Camille earned her bachelor's degree in Mathematics from the University of Texas at Austin. (While at UT, she also lived in the Jester Zoo, rode an Aqua Festival float, and drank hundreds of lattes at Captain Quackenbush's.) In her post-college years, Camille worked as a PC marketing representative (box-kicker) for IBM, and she instructed geometry and calculus to some very wonderful students in Pearsall, Texas. Along the way, she also picked up a masters degree in Curriculum and Instruction from UT San Antonio.

After a fateful interview featuring Tom Jones (the astronaut — not the entertainer), Camille landed a fabulous position producing electronic field trips for NASA. There, she traveled to each field center, creating live television events highlighting the agency's aeronautics and space research. Using everything from swimming robots to CU-SeeMe, Camille employed every conceivable technology to convey cutting edge science to the public.

These days, Camille coordinates the Ready To Learn program for the PBS affiliate in Las Vegas, Nevada, boosting literacy among disadvantaged children. On a typical day you can find her happily singing "I Love Pumpernickel" with rowdy tots and a *Barney ActiMates* character. She also hosts PBS's *Live From . . .* specials, teaches educational computing at UNLV, and builds Authorware training CD-ROMs for the International Gaming Institute.

In her spare time, Camille enjoys marveling at the architecture of the Las Vegas Strip with her spectacular husband Michael, who is an intellectual property and Internet attorney. Camille and Michael are the proud parents of a large brood consisting of two felines (Fritz and Tikka), three canines (Rio, Houdini, and Picasso), and two computers (Micron and Gateway).

Camille is also the author of *PowerPoint 97 For Windows For Dummies Quick Reference* (IDG Books Worldwide, Inc.).

ABOUT IDG BOOKS WORLDWIDE

Welcome to the world of IDG Books Worldwide.

IDG Books Worldwide, Inc., is a subsidiary of International Data Group, the world's largest publisher of computer-related information and the leading global provider of information services on information technology. IDG was founded more than 30 years ago by Patrick J. McGovern and now employs more than 9,000 people worldwide. IDG publishes more than 290 computer publications in over 75 countries. More than 90 million people read one or more IDG publications each month.

Launched in 1990, IDG Books Worldwide is today the #1 publisher of best-selling computer books in the United States. We are proud to have received eight awards from the Computer Press Association in recognition of editorial excellence and three from Computer Currents' First Annual Readers' Choice Awards. Our best-selling ...For Dummies® series has more than 50 million copies in print with translations in 31 languages. IDG Books Worldwide, through a joint venture with IDG's Hi-Tech Beijing, became the first U.S. publisher to publish a computer book in the People's Republic of China. In record time, IDG Books Worldwide has become the first choice for millions of readers around the world who want to learn how to better manage their businesses.

Our mission is simple: Every one of our books is designed to bring extra value and skill-building instructions to the reader. Our books are written by experts who understand and care about our readers. The knowledge base of our editorial staff comes from years of experience in publishing, education, and journalism — experience we use to produce books to carry us into the new millennium. In short, we care about books, so we attract the best people. We devote special attention to details such as audience, interior design, use of icons, and illustrations. And because we use an efficient process of authoring, editing, and desktop publishing our books electronically, we can spend more time ensuring superior content and less time on the technicalities of making books.

You can count on our commitment to deliver high-quality books at competitive prices on topics you want to read about. At IDG Books Worldwide, we continue in the IDG tradition of delivering quality for more than 30 years. You'll find no better book on a subject than one from IDG Books Worldwide.

John Kilcullen
Chairman and CEO
IDG Books Worldwide, Inc.

Steven Berkowitz
President and Publisher
IDG Books Worldwide, Inc.

Eighth Annual
Computer Press
Awards ≥1992

Ninth Annual
Computer Press
Awards ≥1993

Tenth Annual
Computer Press
Awards ≥1994

Eleventh Annual
Computer Press
Awards ≥1995

IDG is the world's leading IT media, research and exposition company. Founded in 1964, IDG had 1997 revenues of $2.05 billion and has more than 9,000 employees worldwide. IDG offers the widest range of media options that reach IT buyers in 75 countries representing 95% of worldwide IT spending. IDG's diverse product and services portfolio spans six key areas including print publishing, online publishing, expositions and conferences, market research, education and training, and global marketing services. More than 90 million people read one or more of IDG's 290 magazines and newspapers, including IDG's leading global brands — Computerworld, PC World, Network World, Macworld and the Channel World family of publications. IDG Books Worldwide is one of the fastest-growing computer book publishers in the world, with more than 700 titles in 36 languages. The "...For Dummies®" series alone has more than 50 million copies in print. IDG offers online users the largest network of technology-specific Web sites around the world through IDG.net (http://www.idg.net), which comprises more than 225 targeted Web sites in 55 countries worldwide. International Data Corporation (IDC) is the world's largest provider of information technology data, analysis and consulting, with research centers in over 41 countries and more than 400 research analysts worldwide. IDG World Expo is a leading producer of more than 168 globally branded conferences and expositions in 35 countries including E3 (Electronic Entertainment Expo), Macworld Expo, ComNet, Windows World Expo, ICE (Internet Commerce Expo), Agenda, DEMO, and Spotlight. IDG's training subsidiary, ExecuTrain, is the world's largest computer training company, with more than 230 locations worldwide and 785 training courses. IDG Marketing Services helps industry-leading IT companies build international brand recognition by developing global integrated marketing programs via IDG's print, online and exposition products worldwide. Further information about the company can be found at www.idg.com.   1/24/99

Dedication

To Michael, for all the hours we sat side by side, clicking away at our computers.

Author's Acknowledgments

First and foremost, I'd like to thank my Project Editor, Mary Goodwin, for doing such a fabulous job of getting this project done fast and done right. Who says you can't do both? I am very grateful for Mary spending countless hours with me on the phone and online, hashing out the many details of taking this book from concept to publication. Mary, you're the best!

My thanks also goes to Associate Acquisitions Editor Steve Hayes — a man who possesses the perfect mix of technical know-how, professionalism, and market awareness. Steve has done such a wonderful job of running logistical interference that I actually think this book-writing gig is easy work!

I also want to thank Technical Editor Jim McCarter for verifying the technical aspects of the book, and Stacey Mickelbart, my Copy Editor, for making me sound great.

I'd also like to acknowledge my managers at KLVX-TV, Lee Solonche and Tom Axtell, for always being so supportive of my creative technology ventures.

Lastly I would like to acknowledge Tony Howard, Glen Sobey, and Louis Gould — teachers who empowered me with skills for writing this book. They may or may not remember me, but I certainly remember them and what they taught me.

Publisher's Acknowledgments

We're proud of this book; please register your comments through our IDG Books Worldwide Online Registration Form located at: http://my2cents.dummies.com.

Some of the people who helped bring this book to market include the following:

Acquisitions, Editorial, and
Media Development

Senior Project Editor: Mary Goodwin
(Previous Edition:
Colleen Williams Esterline)

Associate Acquisitions Editor:
Steven H. Hayes

Copy Editor: Stacey Mickelbart
(Previous Edition: Diane Giangrossi,
Stephanie Koutek)

Technical Editor: Jim McCarter

Associate Permissions Editor:
Carmen Krikorian

Editorial Managers: Kelly Ewing,
Leah P. Cameron

Editorial Assistant: Paul Kuzmic

Production

Project Coordinator: Tom Missler

Layout and Graphics:
Valery Bourke, Linda M. Boyer,
J. Tyler Connor, Maridee V. Ennis,
Angela F. Hunckler, Jane E. Martin,
Brent Savage, Janet Seib, Jacque
Schneider, Brian Taskey

Proofreaders: Kelli Botta, Christine
Sabooni, Rebecca Senninger,
Ethel M. Winslow, Janet M. Withers

Indexer: Sharon Hilgenberg

General and Administrative

IDG Books Worldwide, Inc.: John Kilcullen, CEO; Steven Berkowitz, President and
Publisher

IDG Books Technology Publishing: Brenda McLaughlin, Senior Vice President and
Group Publisher

Dummies Technology Press and Dummies Editorial: Diane Graves Steele, Vice President
and Associate Publisher; Mary Bednarek, Director of Acquisitions and Product
Development; Kristin A. Cocks, Editorial Director

Dummies Trade Press: Kathleen A. Welton, Vice President and Publisher; Kevin Thornton,
Acquisitions Manager

IDG Books Production for Dummies Press: Michael R. Britton, Vice President of
Production and Creative Services; Cindy L. Phipps, Manager of Project
Coordination, Production Proofreading, and Indexing; Kathie S. Schutte,
Supervisor of Page Layout; Shelley Lea, Supervisor of Graphics and Design;
Debbie J. Gates, Production Systems Specialist; Robert Springer, Supervisor of
Proofreading; Debbie Stailey, Special Projects Coordinator; Tony Augsburger,
Supervisor of Reprints and Bluelines

Dummies Packaging and Book Design: Patty Page, Manager, Promotions Marketing

♦

The publisher would like to give special thanks to Patrick J. McGovern,
without whom this book would not have been possible.

♦

Contents at a Glance

Table of Contents

How to Use This Book

Imagine giving your next presentation with dynamic graphics, crisp text, snazzy sounds, and awesome animation. Now imagine not having to stay up all night — or pay a Fort Knox fortune — to create that presentation. That's what PowerPoint is all about: creating high-impact presentations with minimal bother.

Most importantly, you don't need a four-credit college course to master PowerPoint. All you need is this *PowerPoint 2000 For Windows For Dummies Quick Reference,* the perfect guide for answering your PowerPoint "how-do-I's?" No fuss. No boring details; just quick answers to your questions about using the coolest presentation program ever.

How This Book Is Organized

This Quick Reference is divided into several parts for easy search-and-find PowerPoint missions. Within each part, topics are organized alphabetically, and each topic is useable as a stand-alone unit. Don't feel compelled to start on page 1, moving page by page until you reach the *z* entries in the Index. Allow yourself to bypass all material not pertaining directly to the information you seek . . . after all, this is a Quick Reference.

Part I: Getting to Know PowerPoint 2000

This part tells you about the features in PowerPoint and gives you a road map for navigating the program.

Part II: Creating Basic Presentations and Slides

Part II covers the steps involved in building a simple PowerPoint presentation. Part II shows you how to add new slides, format the slides using AutoLayouts and color schemes, and all sorts of other skills you need to create a basic presentation.

Part III: Working with Templates and Masters

Here, you find tips on selecting, editing, and applying templates that control the look of all slides in a presentation. Part III also includes information on manipulating the master documents that dictate the structure of slides, the title slide, audience handouts, and speaker notes.

Part IV: Adding Text

This part serves as your reference for adding text to slides. Find details on creating and formatting text, including font selection, changing text colors, bulleting, bolding and italicizing, spell-checking, finding and replacing text, and setting indents and tabs.

Part V: Adding Multimedia Goodies

Part V explores how you can add real panache to your stash of slides. This part gives the lowdown on incorporating everything from simple drawings to bedazzling sounds and movies to spice up your slides and increase information delivery.

Part VI: Showing Your Business Savvy

Part VI deals with using PowerPoint tools that help you visually express analytical data, procedures, and relationships — the stuff of every good business presentation! You find information on how to build organizational charts and how to convert numerical information into snappy-looking graphs in several formats.

Part VII: Showing Your Presentation

This part helps you with putting the finishing touches on a slide show to make it ready for audience presentation. You can find out how to use slide transitions to reveal slides. Part VII also addresses the physical equipment needed to display your presentation.

Part VIII: Publishing Your Presentation

This part assists you with packaging your PowerPoint presentation in a variety of distribution formats. You find everything you need to know about generating 35mm slides and color and black-and-white transparencies. You can also find information on creating hardcopy printouts of slides used in your presentation — a simple and sharp-looking way to create audience handouts.

Part IX: Using PowerPoint Online

Part IX showcases the incredible online features made available in this latest version of PowerPoint. Among other things, you see how easy it is to convert your PowerPoint presentation into HTML so that it can be published on the Web.

Part X: Tips, Tricks, and Troubleshooting

Assorted odds and ends, such as file management and time-saving tips, are covered in this part. You also find out what to do when good presentations go bad.

Icons Used in This Book

Much like the AutoBahn, it's a good idea to post universally accepted road signs to guide your travel down the PowerPoint highway. I know you plan on flipping fast and furious through the following pages, and these handy icons will help focus your attention as you navigate to the information you seek.

Points you to special information that makes your life much easier.

Alerts you to potential PowerPoint disasters that can ruin your presentation. Think, "Danger, Will Robinson!"

Sends you to another ...For Dummies book if you need extra guidance or information.

Informs you of the most expedient way to accomplish a task.

Says, "Yes, I know this procedure seems illogical and counter-intuitive, but this is how Microsoft set up this silly program anyway."

Getting to Know PowerPoint 2000

Say goodbye to dreary ol' presentation media like whiteboards and viewgraphs. Say hello to ultra-professional looking PowerPoint visuals built in bodacious colors and embellished with eye-popping text, graphics, charts, and movies!

In this part, I help you integrate common PowerPoint terms like *new slide* and *insert sound* into your daily vocabulary. I also show you how to perform a few tasks that you need to do almost every time you open and work in a PowerPoint presentation.

In this part . . .

- ✔ Changing views
- ✔ Closing a presentation and PowerPoint
- ✔ Getting help
- ✔ Opening a PowerPoint presentation
- ✔ Saving your work
- ✔ Updating old PowerPoint files
- ✔ Using buttons and bars

About Slides

PowerPoint presentations are comprised of *slides*. In many ways, your audiences view PowerPoint slides in a similar fashion to the way they view regular 35mm slides projected from a slide carousel. But making and showing PowerPoint slides is much easier, faster, and much more functional than 35mm slides.

Showing PowerPoint slides is also much more exciting than clicking through traditional slides. That's because PowerPoint can include text, graphics, movies, and audio clips all presented in animated steps to convey your information in a precise, engaging sequence. It can also include television-quality cuts and fades between slides.

So what does a PowerPoint slide actually look like? I'm glad you asked! Basically, a slide looks like anything you want it to look like. Sometimes it looks like a simple piece of text — like your company mission statement. Other times it looks like a list of bulleted items — like ingredients for guacamole — that fly in animated steps, one bullet item at a time, onto the slide. And other times it looks like a graph of product sales forecasts or a labeled diagram of earthworm innards. If you can dream it up, you can probably stick it on a slide and show it to your audience.

Changing Your View

Next to the horizontal scroll bar sits a collection of buttons from which you can choose your view. You can also choose a view by clicking the <u>V</u>iew menu from the Menu bar. You can work on your PowerPoint presentation in any of the following views:

- ✦ **Normal view:** A combination of Slide view and Outline view. Shows three panes simultaneously — your presentation outline on the left, your slide on the right, and your speaker notes at the bottom. *See also* Part II for more information on working in Normal view.

- ✦ **Slide view:** Shows a single slide under construction. You're able to see all text, colors, pictures, sounds, and movies in the view. This view allows you to create and edit all information and images on your slides. *See also* Part II for more information on working in Slide view.

- ✦ **Outline view:** Shows an ordered list of the text information on your slides. In Outline view, you can examine the entire text content of your presentation all at once. This view allows you to create and edit text information on your slides, but it does not let you add or edit non-text items such as clip art. This view also gives you a cute thumbnail sketch of your slide beside its associated outline position. *See also* Part II for more information on working in Outline view.

 ✦ **Slide Sorter view:** Shows thumbnails of all your slides simultaneously, neatly presented in orderly rows and columns. Slide Sorter view enables you to quickly change the order of your slides by dragging and dropping them into new positions. *See also* Part II for more information on working in Slide Sorter view.

 ✦ **Slide Show view:** Presents the completed stack of slides to a viewing audience. *See also* Part VII for in-depth coverage on using Slide Show view.

Exiting a Presentation and PowerPoint

When it's time to close up shop, kick back for the evening, and bask in a little Microsoft glory, close the PowerPoint files that you're working on in either of the following ways:

✦ Choose File⇨Close.

✦ Press Ctrl+W.

 You don't need to close your files if you're going to exit the program. You may instead simply exit PowerPoint, and the program saves your work and closes your presentation as it shuts down. You can say goodbye to PowerPoint in any of the following ways:

✦ Choose File⇨Exit.

✦ Click the Close box at the top-right corner of the PowerPoint window.

✦ Press Alt+F4.

PowerPoint doesn't let you quit without asking if you want to save changes. Answer politely to complete the exiting process.

Getting Help

PowerPoint 2000 offers an assortment of handy help tools to aid you through the stumbling blocks along your presentation-building route.

Using the Office Assistant

The most useful — and also the most playful — help tool in PowerPoint is a tiny cartoon character called the Office Assistant. The Assistant appears to float above your PowerPoint window. You can easily move the Assistant by clicking it and dragging it to a new location.

You can open the Assistant by using any of these methods:

✦ Choose Help➪Microsoft PowerPoint Help from the Menu bar.

 ✦ Click the Microsoft PowerPoint Help button on the Standard toolbar.

✦ Press F1.

 You can easily turn off the Assistant — if it gets too feisty — by right-clicking the mouse and selecting Hide from the pop-up menu. Ask it to rematerialize by clicking the Microsoft PowerPoint Help button on the Standard toolbar.

The Assistant initially appears as an animated paper clip named Clippit, but you can change it to any one of several other characters. My personal favorite is Rocky, the dog — however, I'm also partial to the Genius (Einstein, of course!). To hire a different Assistant, follow these steps:

1. Open the Assistant by choosing Help➪Microsoft PowerPoint Help from the Menu bar.

2. Right-click the Assistant and select Choose Assistant from the pop-up menu. An Office Assistant dialog box appears with the Gallery tab selected.

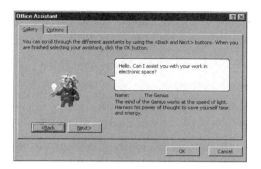

3. Browse the Gallery by clicking Next or Back until you find an Assistant you like.

4. Click OK to accept your choice of Assistant.

You may have to insert the PowerPoint CD-ROM to install the selected Office Assistant.

Each time you call upon the Assistant, it asks you to type a word or two to describe what you want to know. After you tell the Assistant what to look for, it searches the Help files and provides a short list of topics that may match your description. Clicking the help topic that most closely matches what you need displays a window showing detailed help information.

The Assistant may also provide, at the bottom of the list of help topics, the option None of the above, look for more help on the Web. Pressing this option connects you to online help where you can search the extensive Microsoft Office database for the help you need.

You may find the Assistant helpful not only for responding to your queries, but also for anticipating questions you may have while working in PowerPoint. The Assistant is a good mind reader, and it often sprouts a lightbulb overhead whenever it thinks you may need a little guidance. Click once on the lightbulb to see what helpful idea the Assistant has in mind.

The Office Assistant dialog box offers an Options tab that allows you to fine-tune many details of how and when the Assistant provides help.

Using the Internet

PowerPoint also offers help via the Internet by providing a direct link to the Microsoft Office Update Web site. But you need to have an Internet connection to use this nifty feature! To use online help, choose Help⊏>Office on the Web from the Menu bar. Choosing this help option launches your Web browser and transports you directly to a Web site called Office Update.

Many support features are available from the Office Update Web site, but you may find these two areas most worthwhile to visit:

✦ **Search:** This area is a searchable database of technical information about all of the Microsoft programs, PowerPoint included. Office Update Search serves a similar role as PowerPoint's Help feature, but the online information is much more comprehensive and up-to-date.

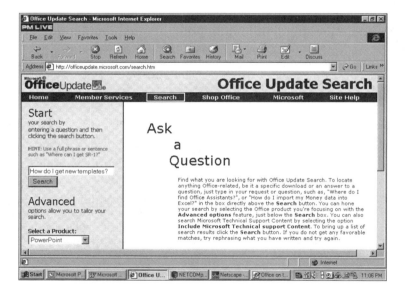

✦ **Home⊏>PowerPoint:** Choosing Home from the Office Update page leads you to a page where you can get information on any Microsoft program. Choosing PowerPoint from the Home page takes you to the following helpful areas:

• **Assistance:** Includes extra clip art, FAQs, and newsgroups. FAQs are "Frequently Asked Questions" — and answers — about PowerPoint. This is a good place to go if you believe you're asking something that many other people have probably asked at some point.

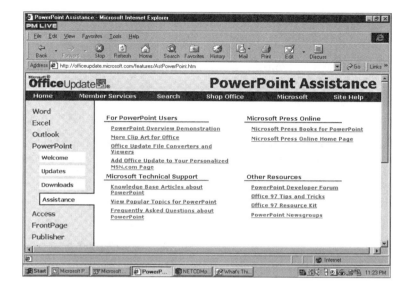

- **Newsgroups:** Provides access to Microsoft-sponsored Internet discussion groups about PowerPoint. This area is ideal for asking the quirky questions you believe may require an expert to figure out. Simply post a question to the group, and a few hours (or days) later, someone in the know will respond with an answer.

Using the What's This? Pointer

The What's This? option is a nifty little help tool that enables you to point to items on-screen and ask, "What's This?" Enabling What's This? replaces your normal arrow pointer with a special "question pointer" that helps you get quick and easy answers to many PowerPoint questions without searching through Help menus.

You can summon What's This? by using either of these methods:

✦ Choose Help➪What's This? from the Menu bar.

✦ Press Shift+F1.

 Your pointer suddenly sprouts a small question mark on its side. Move the pointer to any item on-screen — such as a button on a toolbar — and click. A pop-up box appears with a brief explanation of the selected item's function or purpose. And your pointer returns to its normal appearance.

Moving around in PowerPoint 2000

You move through PowerPoint 2000 by using the same methods you find in other Microsoft programs.

Using the keyboard

The keyboard attached to your computer probably looks and functions much the same way as a trusty old typewriter, with a couple of exceptions. Besides not having to bang the keys with finger-exhausting power, your computer keyboard also offers extra keys that provide a variety of helpful functions. The following table offers a sampling of what you can do with your keyboard.

Key	Action It Performs
Esc	Backs you out of menu or dialog box commands and halts a slide show in progress.
F1–F12	Provides shortcut functions for a variety of menu commands.
Delete	Cuts the currently highlighted text, the selected object, or the character to the right of the cursor.
Home	Takes you to the first slide in your presentation, in any view.
End	Takes you to the last slide in your presentation, in any view.
Insert	Switches between inserting and overstriking (replacing) characters while you edit text.
PgUp	Takes you one slide back in your presentation, in any view.
PgDn	Takes you one slide forward in your presentation, in any view.
Left, up arrows	Moves you one animation step backwards in your presentation during a slide show. Moves you backwards through your slides in Slide Sorter view.
Right, down arrows	Moves you one animation step forward in your presentation during a slide show. Moves you forward through your slides in Slide Sorter view.

Using the mouse

The mouse operates the on-screen pointer, which is used for selecting objects, moving them around, and other necessary activities.

When you look on your screen, you notice a pointer that indicates your position on-screen and changes shape depending on the job it's available to perform. When the pointer appears as an arrow, you can use it to select something. When it appears as a double-headed arrow, you can use it to resize something. And when it appears as an I-beam, you can use the pointer to type or edit text.

The mouse itself has two buttons, one on the left and another on the right. Much of the time you click one of these buttons or click and hold a button as you drag the mouse over the mouse pad. Sometimes you need to double-click the mouse, which means to click the left button two times in rapid succession. You may want to start muscling-up your right index finger as you may find you spend significantly more time left-clicking and doubling-clicking than right-clicking.

Opening a Presentation

After firing up PowerPoint (by choosing Programs⇨Microsoft PowerPoint in the Start menu), you see the start-up PowerPoint dialog box.

The PowerPoint dialog box provides four choices to begin developing your PowerPoint presentation:

+ **AutoContent Wizard:** The Wizard yields a nearly complete set of PowerPoint slides. You just need to supply the Wizard with some basic lines of text, let the Wizard do its thing, and then you can tweak the final product.

+ **Design Template:** This option provides you with cool pre-designed layouts that still offer you the flexibility to alter the layout elements.

+ **Blank presentation:** Gives you blank slides with no color and no artwork, which is great for the minimalists and artists. Allows you to build a really barren stack of slides (good for black and white transparencies), or you can create all your artistic elements from scratch.

+ **Open an existing presentation:** Allows you to go back and work on any presentation that you previously named and saved.

You also have the option of clicking to select the check box for Don't show this dialog box again. If you do so, you have to choose File⇨New to open a new presentation each time you run PowerPoint.

See also Part II for more information about using these options.

Saving Your Work

While composing an award-winning presentation or lecture, you certainly want to save your work. Save often. If you close your file or exit PowerPoint without saving your slides, consider them gone forever. Saving often also buys you insurance against losing everything in the event you have a power surge or if your computer crashes.

Save your goods by using one of the following methods:

+ Click the Save button on the Standard toolbar.

+ Choose File⇨Save.

+ Press Ctrl+S or Shift+F12.

The first time you save a presentation, the Save As dialog box appears for you to type in the name of your newly created file. You may notice that the Save As dialog box includes a Places bar on the left-hand side showing locations where you may want to save your file. Options on the Places bar include History, My Documents, Desktop, Favorites, and Web Folders. You can also click the down-arrow beside the Save in area to locate another folder that you want to save your file to.

Each time you save after the initial save, PowerPoint automatically saves your file with the same name — and in the same location — as it did with your initial save.

Type a name for your presentation in the File name area. In the Save as type area, choose Presentation to save your file as a PowerPoint 2000 presentation. Some other Save as type options include Web Page, PowerPoint 95, PowerPoint 97-2000 & 95, and PowerPoint 4.0.

+ Saving as a Web Page converts your file to the HTML language necessary to display your file on the World Wide Web. If you save your file as a Web page, you may notice that PowerPoint actually saves two items to your destination folder: a file full of graphics, sounds, movies, and an index created from your presentation, as well as a shortcut to the browser page for viewing your Web presentation. *See also* Part IX for more about working with PowerPoint online.

+ Saving as an earlier version of PowerPoint — PowerPoint 95, PowerPoint 97-2000 & 95, or PowerPoint 4.0 — allows you to open your presentation with an earlier version of PowerPoint. This is a great option if you plan on showing your presentation on a computer not yet upgraded to PowerPoint 2000. Be aware, though, that saving as an earlier version causes some of the bells and whistles of PowerPoint 2000 to be lost.

Updating Old PowerPoint Files

You can easily convert a presentation from an older version of PowerPoint to PowerPoint 2000. Just boot up PowerPoint 2000 and open your old presentation from inside the File menu. A serious-looking message appears warning you that the file will be opened as read-only. Finish the update conversion by saving the file with a new name.

After the file is saved with a new name, it is no longer read-only, and you can make changes and resave as needed.

Using Buttons and Bars

Like most Windows-based programs, you operate PowerPoint by using a handful of buttons and toolbars. Most of the time you view the buttons and bars as they appear in Normal view — the view that enables you to see each slide under construction, along with the outline of your presentation and your speaker notes.

If you've ever used computer software in your life (at least in the post-DOS years), I bet that many of these buttons and bars look familiar to you. The following list gives you a quick tour of the many buttons and bars available for your use:

+ **Title bar:** Tells you the name of the presentation you're working on when the presentation window is maximized. Otherwise, the program Title bar shows the words *Microsoft PowerPoint.* Text on the Title bar appears in white text on a blue background at the very top of the PowerPoint window.

+ **Menu bar:** Sits just below the Title bar. It offers a variety of menus which allow you to control most functions of the PowerPoint program.

+ **Toolbars:** Offer you buttons for some of the most commonly used operations from the menus on the Menu bar.

  • **Standard toolbar:** Features frequently-used actions such as save, print, spell-check, and zoom.

  • **Formatting and Drawing toolbars:** Help you put words and pictures on your slides.

Display additional toolbars by choosing <u>V</u>iew⇨<u>T</u>oolbars from the Menu bar and clicking to check the toolbars that you want to show.

✦ **Scroll bars:** Two scroll bars border the slide work area: one on the right and one on the bottom. Pressing the arrows at the ends of the scroll bars adjusts your viewing perspective of the slide work area. You can also click directly in the scroll bar, or click and drag the elevator box in the scroll bar to move through your work area.

✦ **Status bar:** Indicates which slide you're working on at any given time, and what design template you are using.

✦ **View buttons:** Give you different ways of viewing your PowerPoint slides. *See also* "Changing Your View" in this part.

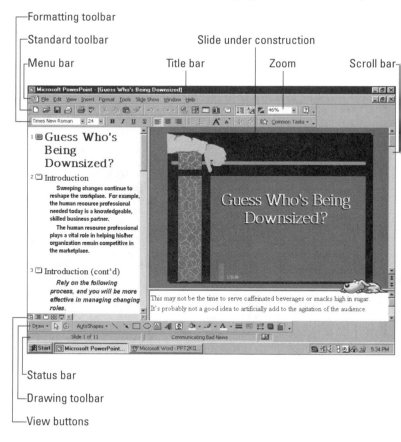

You can customize the buttons on a toolbar by clicking the More Buttons button at the right-hand end of a toolbar. Clicking this button causes an Add or Remove Button menu to appear. Select the Add or Remove Buttons menu item, and a menu of PowerPoint buttons appears. Click to place a check next to each button you want added to the toolbar. Press Reset Toolbar on this menu to revert the toolbar to its original contents. Press Customize to add buttons not listed on the menu. Pressing Customize opens a Customize dialog box where you can click a button and drag it to any toolbar you want.

 Still confused about the whole business of buttons and bars? Then tread back to your bookstore and nab a copy of *Windows 95 For Dummies,* 2nd Edition, or *Windows 98 For Dummies,* both by Andy Rathbone (IDG Books Worldwide, Inc.). And call me in the morning.

Part II

Creating Basic Presentations and Slides

This part covers the basic steps that you need to know to create slides and presentations. I also tell you how to work in some of the views that PowerPoint offers.

In this part . . .

- ✓ Starting a new presentation
- ✓ Working with slides
- ✓ Getting acquainted with Outline view
- ✓ Working in Slide Sorter view
- ✓ Opening saved presentations

Beginning a New Presentation

Every time you start the PowerPoint program, a PowerPoint dialog box appears and offers you the option of opening a new presentation. To begin a new presentation, simply click Blank presentation, Design Template, or AutoContent wizard, and then click OK. Clicking Blank presentation opens a new blank presentation in PowerPoint. If you click Design Template or AutoContent wizard, a New Presentation dialog box appears, and you must make some design choices before your new presentation actually opens.

If you already have PowerPoint up and running, you can use either of these methods to start a new presentation:

✦ **Choose File⇨New from the Menu bar:** You see a New Presentation dialog box with tabs providing options for generating your presentation. (Don't be surprised that the New Presentation dialog box looks very different than the PowerPoint dialog box.)

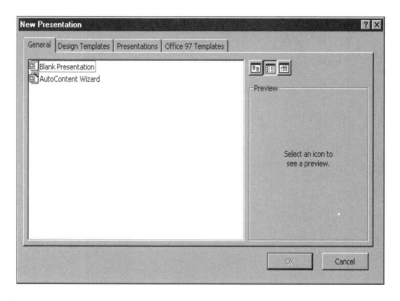

✦ **Press Ctrl+N:** PowerPoint automatically creates a new blank presentation and displays the New Slide dialog box.

The tabs that you see in the New Presentation dialog box depend upon whether you have ever installed a prior version of

PowerPoint on your computer. You always see the General, Design Templates, and Presentations tabs. If you have previously installed PowerPoint 97, you see a tab labeled Office 97 Templates. If you have previously installed PowerPoint 95, you see a tab labeled Office 95 Templates. And if you have previously installed both PowerPoint 95 and PowerPoint 97, you see tabs for templates from each of those versions.

When opening a new PowerPoint presentation, your work area always appears in Normal view — the three-pane window showing your slide, outline, and notes simultaneously. If you save a presentation in some other view, such as Outline or Slide Sorter, PowerPoint reopens the presentation in the view being used at the time of the most recent save. *See also* Part I for more information on the different views in PowerPoint.

Creating a blank presentation

Choose Blank Presentation from the PowerPoint dialog box or from the General tab of the New Presentation dialog box to begin with blank slides (no color and no artwork).

Blank presentations can still provide placeholders for adding text and graphic objects, but they are otherwise barren of images, colors, or artistic design. Blank presentations are ideal for building complete layouts from scratch or for creating simple, text-only presentations. (Text-only presentations can be printed inexpensively in black ink on overhead transparencies to create a back-up presentation option.)

Creating a presentation with templates

Choosing Design Template from the PowerPoint dialog box or choosing any non-General tab from the New Presentation dialog box means that you have to shop from a folder full of pretty designs before singling out one that catches your eye. Design Templates and Office Templates (if you have them) offer visually appealing colors and design elements *only,* while Presentations goes one step further by offering suggested content for common presentation themes.

You have Office Templates only if you installed a previous version of PowerPoint before installing PowerPoint 2000.

On all of the templates tabs, clicking the name of any template yields a thumbnail sketch of how the design appears on your computer screen.

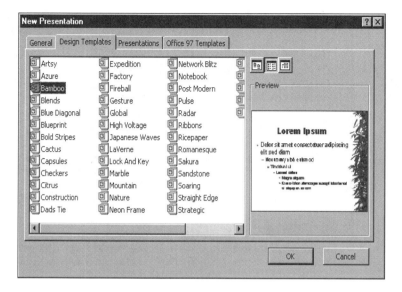

Pick a style that suits your fancy and then click OK to accept it. The New Slide dialog box appears and asks you to choose an AutoLayout for your first slide.

Creating a presentation with the wizard

The wizard is a simple program that builds a rudimentary set of PowerPoint slides based on a few tidbits of information you input to the program. The wizard is a good way to get started with PowerPoint, but don't be fooled into thinking that it magically does all the work for you — it doesn't. Just accept the wizard for what it is — a quick and dirty way to generate a basic set of PowerPoint slides.

To create a presentation using the wizard, just follow these steps:

1. Start PowerPoint. If you already started PowerPoint, choose New from the Menu bar.

2. At the start-up PowerPoint dialog box or New Presentation dialog box, click AutoContent Wizard and click OK. The AutoContent Wizard is located under the General tab in the New Presentation dialog box.

3. Click Next. The wizard now asks you a series of questions.

4. Choose a presentation type from the list and then click Next. Your choices consist of All, General, Corporate, Projects, Sales/Marketing, and Carnegie Coach.

5. Choose a presentation style from the list; then click <u>N</u>ext.

Presentation style choices include On-<u>s</u>creen presentation, W<u>e</u>b presentation, Black-and-<u>w</u>hite overheads, <u>C</u>olor overheads, or <u>3</u>5mm slides. Choose On-<u>s</u>creen presentation if you plan on presenting in front of an audience (face-to-face) or via a computer-networked meeting. Choose W<u>e</u>b presentation if you plan to post your slides to the Web for online access. Choose overheads if you want to print transparencies to use with an overhead projector. And choose <u>3</u>5mm slides if you want to show your presentation using a traditional slide carousel.

6. Complete the presentation options dialog box by typing a <u>P</u>resentation title.

You can also type a <u>F</u>ooter and click in the appropriate check boxes to have the <u>D</u>ate last updated and the <u>S</u>lide number placed on each slide.

7. Click <u>N</u>ext. The wizard presents a final wrap-up screen.

8. Click <u>F</u>inish. Your presentation appears on-screen in Normal view.

Creating and Working with Slides

Slides are the fundamental building blocks of a PowerPoint presentation. All the information in your presentation appears either directly on a slide or is attached to a slide as reference material. This section assists you in creating slides and moving around a collection of slides in a presentation.

Adding a new slide

When you begin a new presentation — except for a presentation created with an AutoContent Wizard — PowerPoint provides you with one spanking-fresh slide to work with. (New presentations created with an AutoContent Wizard may provide you with ten or more slides to contend with.) However, unless you are the most painfully concise human on the planet, I imagine you want more than a single slide in your PowerPoint presentation.

You can add a new slide in any view except Slide Show view. *See also* Part I for more information on the different views in PowerPoint.

To add a new slide to your presentation, you can do any of the following:

♦ Click the New Slide button on the Standard toolbar.

♦ Click the Common Tasks button on the Formatting toolbar and then click the New Slide button.

♦ Choose Insert⇨New Slide from the Menu bar.

♦ Press Ctrl+M.

Each time you add a new slide, you're presented with a New Slide dialog box.

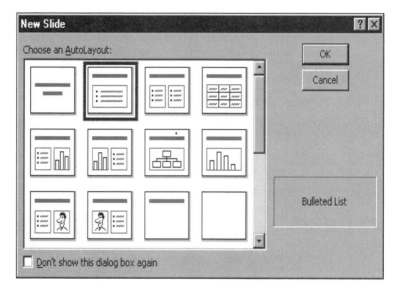

The New Slide dialog box contains 24 *AutoLayouts,* which are slide layouts that PowerPoint automatically sets up for you. The AutoLayouts offer various combinations of title slides, text bullets, clip art, and other features. If you want to fully customize the slide yourself, choose the blank slide option.

Each new slide can be created using a different AutoLayout, allowing you to create a presentation with a variety of formats tailored to meet your specific needs.

Typing text on the slide

Each new slide that you create reserves a partitioned zone where you can type your text (except for when you choose to create a completely blank slide). These "type here" zones are called *text boxes.*

Notice that the placeholders Click to add title, Click to add subtitle, or Click to add text occupy the text boxes until you replace the boxes with your own words.

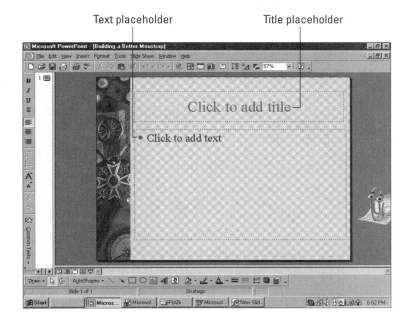

Text placeholder · Title placeholder

Moving the cursor into a text box converts the cursor from an arrow to an I-beam, indicating that the text box is ready to accept text. When this happens, click the mouse anywhere in the box (the place you click is your text insertion point) and start typing. Now PowerPoint acts like a word processor. The left and right arrow keys move you around, and the Delete key erases your typing.

Keep the following in mind when you enter text on a slide:

✦ You may often want to type a title in one text box (the title area), followed by a few text bullets in another text box located just below the title (the object area). Just click in the box where you want to add text and type away.

✦ You can delete text boxes if you have no interest in filling them in. To delete a text box, click anywhere in the text box; then click the edge of the text box (avoid clicking the sizing handle dots) and press the Delete key.

✦ You can type on some other part of the slide outside the text boxes. Click the Text Box button on the Drawing toolbar and then click outside the existing text boxes to create a new text box. You can now type at the insertion point inside the new text box.

✦ Words automatically wrap when they reach the right border of a text box, but if you want to move immediately to the next line, press Enter. *See also* Part IV for more information about handling text.

PowerPoint tries to fit any text you type within the boundaries of the text placeholder. If the amount of text you type can't fit in the boundaries comfortably, PowerPoint decreases the point size of the text to create a better fit. To turn this feature off, choose Tools➪Options from the Menu bar to summon the Options dialog box. Click the Edit tab, and then click to clear the Auto-fit text to text placeholder check box.

Pasting clip art onto a new slide

Every so often, you may want to add a relevant picture that "tells the story" to your slides. You may choose to add clip art, photos, drawings, or scanned images to your slides — the possibilities are endless!

The simplest way to add a picture to a new slide is to grab one out of the Microsoft Clip Gallery that accompanies PowerPoint. Just follow these steps:

 1. Insert a new slide into your presentation by clicking the New Slide button or pressing Ctrl+M.

 2. In the New Slide dialog box, select an AutoLayout that includes a clip art placeholder. This doesn't limit you to only adding pictures in the form of clip art — "clip art placeholder" is just an old and beloved name for the type of AutoLayout that includes a picture. You can actually add any image — a photograph, a scanned drawing, a piece of clip art — when using this AutoLayout.

 3. Double-click the placeholder to open the Microsoft Clip Gallery's catalog of pictures.

 4. Click a picture category (such as Business or Travel) and then click a picture in that category.

 5. Click the Insert Clip button from the pop-up menu that accompanies your selected picture. Your chosen image is magically glued to your slide.

See also Part V for additional details on adding pictures and other goodies to your slides.

Using a color scheme

Color schemes let you alter slide background colors, text colors, and accent colors. For each scheme, PowerPoint provides you with eight coordinated colors that complement one another in an aesthetically pleasing combination. The schemes ensure that the colors match and that text readability is maximized relative to the background.

Schemes offer light-on-dark combinations, dark-on-light combinations, bolds, brights, pastels, and neutrals. The same schemes can also be used to color charts and tables and to recolor pictures.

You can get a look at all your color scheme options at any time, in any view except Slide Show view. To look at color scheme options, choose Format⇔Slide Color Scheme from the Menu bar. This opens the Color Scheme dialog box.

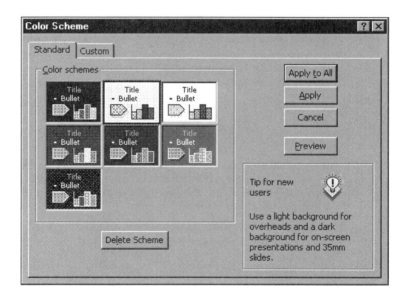

The Color Scheme dialog box has two tabs: Standard and Custom. It also has a Preview button that lets you try on how your Color Scheme choice looks on your very own slides — prior to actually applying the scheme. Each tab does offers the following options:

✦ **Standard tab:** This tab offers a selection of premade Color schemes. Click the Color schemes you want for the current slide and then click Apply. To apply the selected Color scheme to the entire presentation, click Apply to All.

✦ **Custom tab:** This tab allows you to create your own color scheme. In the Scheme colors area, you can change the individual colors of the following items: Background, Text and lines, Shadows, Title text, Fills, Accent, Accent and hyperlink, and Accent and followed hyperlink. To change an individual color, click the color, select Change Color, and then choose a new color in the dialog box that appears and click OK. After making your changes, click the Apply button to make the changes effective on the current slide only, or click the Apply to All button to make the changes effective on all slides in your presentation.

To save a scheme created within the Custom tab area of the Color Scheme dialog box, click Add as Standard Scheme after making your individual color choices. Your new scheme is added to the Standard tab of the Color Scheme dialog box.

Duplicating a slide

Duplicating a slide is an easy way to reuse the formatting of one slide as a guide for other slides. You may find duplicating particularly useful for churning out slides that have the same title and images with variations only on bullet items.

You may also find duplicating a simple way to build a series of steps in a sequence: Just build the entire sequence on a slide, make a duplicate for each step, and then delete the items on each slide that don't belong.

To duplicate a slide, choose Edit⇨Duplicate from the Menu bar, or press Ctrl+D. The currently selected slide is duplicated and placed immediately following its original slide. You are moved to the duplicate slide in the presentation.

If more than one slide is selected, every slide in the selection is duplicated and placed immediately following the last selected slide.

Deleting a slide

Eliminating a slide can be accomplished in any view except Slide Show view. To trash a slide you no longer want, just follow these steps:

1. Select the slide to be deleted by clicking it or moving to the slide in Normal view or Slide view. To select multiple slides, move to Outline or Slide Sorter view, press the Shift key, and click each slide to be deleted.

2. Delete your selection by choosing Edit⇨Cut. You can also press the Backspace or Delete key to delete selected slides.

Moving between slides

You can move from slide to slide during the construction of your PowerPoint presentation in several ways:

✦ **In Normal view or Slide view:** Click the slide number you wish to move to in the Outline pane. You can also:

- Click an arrow on the scroll bar at the right side of the slide pane. The up arrow takes you toward your first slide. The down arrow takes you toward your last slide.

- Use the double arrows to move one slide at a time through your entire set of slides. Dragging the scroll box up or down between the arrows indicates your current slide position in the stack.

- Press PgUp or PgDn to move through your stack one slide at a time.

✦ **In Slide Sorter view:** Double-click the slide that you want to move to.

Opening a Saved Presentation

After you construct and save a presentation, you'll need to open it (at some later time) for display. You may also wish to reopen the presentation for further editing, or to add some additional slides.

PowerPoint offers you the flexibility of saving presentations to — and opening presentations from — a variety of locations. If you're like most users, you may frequently save files to and open files from your own hard drive or possibly a network drive shared by you and your fellow cubicle-dwellers.

Open a saved PowerPoint presentation as follows:

1. Click the Open button on the Standard toolbar, choose File⇨Open from the Menu bar, or press Ctrl+O. The Open dialog box appears.

2. Locate the presentation you want to open in the Places bar or the Look in box. The Places bar is located on the left side of the Open dialog box; it contains several folders that may contain the file you seek.

3. Click the presentation you want to open. A thumbnail picture of the first slide in the presentation you select appears.

4. Press the Open button to open the presentation, or press the arrow next to the Open button for special options in opening the presentation. Special options include Open Read-only,

Open as Copy, and Open in Browser. (For more information about Open in Browser, **see also** Part IX.)

 Files you have used recently are listed under History on the Places bar.

Working in Outline View

In Outline view, your entire presentation appears as an outline shaving the titles and body text from each slide. You still see the Slide pane and the Notes pane, but the size of the Outline pane is maximized relative to the other two.

🗐 Switch to Outline view by clicking the Outline view button, located in the bottom-left hand corner of the PowerPoint window.

The purpose of Outline view is to concentrate on the text of your slides; you can edit text content, text formatting, and text organization. The benefit of working in Outline view is that it lets you easily see how information progresses from slide to slide. And just so you don't forget, the slide pane still shows the aesthetics of how each slide looks during the slide show.

You can create new presentation in the Outline view, or you can switch to Outline view to persue any existing PowerPoint presentation. You can move back and forth among Outline view and all other PowerPoint views at any time as you build and edit your presentations.

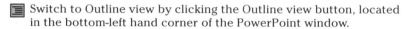 Brainstorming the content of a new presentation is most easily accomplished in Outline view. You can quickly create slide after slide of key concepts by using Outline view as your construction mode; then later switch to Slide view to finesse the look of each slide.

How slides and text are organized

In Outline view, as in Normal view, slides are listed vertically, from the first slide to the last. Each slide is designated by a number and a slide marker.

The slide title appears to the right of each slide marker, and body text, indented up to five levels, appears below the slide title. The body text may appear as paragraphs or bullet items and can be easily moved — rearranged within a slide, or moved to other slides. Some repositioning tasks are accomplished by clicking and dragging the selected slide or text, and others are performed using buttons on the Outlining toolbar.

The Outlining toolbar

When working in Outline view or Normal view, you may want to summon an Outlining toolbar containing specialized buttons for working with the outline of your presentation. Call up the Outlining toolbar by choosing View⇨Toolbars from the Menu bar and clicking to place a check mark by Outlining.

Outlining buttons on the toolbar deal primarily with repositioning text so that the text's significance is appropriately conveyed by its position relative to other text. For example, the Outlining buttons let you move text bullets higher or lower on a bulleted list. Outlining buttons also let you move a bulleted item of text to become a major bullet (this is called promoting text) or a minor bullet (this is called demoting text).

Buttons on the Outlining toolbar include the following:

✦ **Promote:** Elevates the position of the selected paragraph or bullet item by moving it up and left one heading level. For example, makes a level two heading into a level one heading.

✦ **Demote:** Diminishes the position of the selected paragraph or bullet item by moving it down and right one heading level. For example, makes a level two heading into a level three heading.

✦ **Move Up:** Repositions the selected paragraph or bullet item — and any collapsed subordinate text — up, above the preceding displayed paragraph or bullet item. For example, makes the second bullet item on a list become the first bullet item.

Promote
Demote   Summary Slide
Move Up   Show Formatting
Move Down

Expand All
Collapse All
Expand
Collapse

✦ **Move Down:** Repositions the selected paragraph — and any collapsed subordinate text — down, below the following displayed paragraph. For example, makes the second bullet item on a list become the third bullet item.

✦ **Collapse:** Hides body text to show only the title of the selected slide or slides. A slide with collapsed text has a thin gray line underlining its title.

✦ **Expand:** Redisplays collapsed text of selected slides.

✦ **Collapse All:** Collapses the body text of all slides in the presentation.

✦ **Expand All:** Shows the body text of all slides in the presentation.

✦ **Summary Slide:** Builds a new slide from the titles of selected slides. The title of the new slide is Summary Slide, and the summary slide is inserted in front of the first selected slide (serving more as an agenda slide than a summary slide).

✦ **Show Formatting:** Toggles on or off to show or hide text formatting (such as font and point size) in Outline view.

Many of the frequently used Outlining buttons also appear on other toolbars, including the Formatting and the Standard toolbars.

Creating a new presentation

To create a new presentation in Outline view

1. Choose File⇨New from the Menu bar.

2. Choose a presentation type from the New Presentation dialog box. Click OK.

3. Choose an AutoLayout from the New Slide dialog box. An empty slide marker for Slide 1 appears.

4. Click the Outline view button.

5. Type a title for Slide 1 and press Enter.

6. Click the Demote button on the Outlining toolbar, or press Enter and Tab to create the first bullet level. Type text for the first bullet and press Enter. Continue typing and pressing Enter to create as many bullet items as you want.

7. After the final bullet item, press Ctrl+Enter or press Enter and click the Promote button on the Outlining toolbar to create the next slide.

8. Repeat Steps 3 through 7 to create as many slides as you want.

9. Choose File⇨Save from the Menu bar or click the Save button on the Standard toolbar. Type a name for your presentation in the Save in area and click Save.

You can press a different view button at any time to examine how your presentation looks in other views.

Changing the position of a title or paragraph

You can change the position of a slide title or paragraph by following these steps:

1. In Outline view or Normal view, select the title or paragraph you wish to move.

2. Drag the selected text to a new position, or click Promote, Demote, Move Up, or Move Down to reposition the selected text.

Changing the slide order

To move an entire slide to a different position in the outline, follow these steps:

1. In Outline view or Normal view, click and hold the slide marker representing the slide you want to move. The pointer changes to a compass when it moves over the slide marker.

The text of the entire slide — title and body text — is now selected.

2. Drag the selected slide to a new position and let it go, or click Move Up or Move Down to reposition the selected text.

The entire presentation of slides reorders to reflect the repositioning of the moved slide.

Working in Slide Sorter View

During the slide-construction process, you spend most of your time working in Slide view. The limitation of Slide view, however, is that you can't peruse your entire batch of slides simultaneously. Enter Slide Sorter view.

You use Slide Sorter view in the same way that you use a light table to view 35mm slides: Slide Sorter view allows you to inspect all the slides at once and sort them into a sequence that you feel works best for the presentation.

To get into Slide Sorter view from any view, at any slide in your presentation, click the Slide Sorter view button, located with the other view buttons in the lower-left corner of the screen. Or choose <u>V</u>iew⇨Sli<u>d</u>e Sorter.

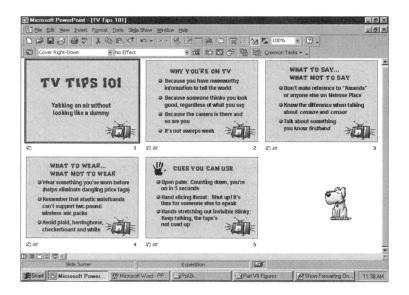

If your entire slide stack doesn't fit on-screen, you may need to use the scroll bars to scroll through your slides.

Also, you can adjust the total number of slides visible in Slide Sorter view by clicking the Zoom drop-down list box on the Standard toolbar.

You can also do a number of other things in Slide Sorter view using the Slide Sorter toolbar.

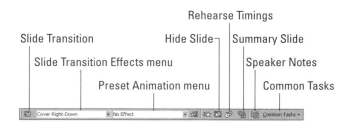

Rehearse Timings

Slide Transition   Hide Slide┐ Summary Slide

Slide Transition Effects menu   Speaker Notes

Preset Animation menu   Common Tasks

The toolbar gives you complete control over several aspects of your presentation — from how each slide appears and disappears (slide transitions) to how bulleted text items and multimedia elements make an entrance onto each slide. You can make use of the following items on the Slide Sorter toolbar:

✦ **Slide Transition button:** Opens the Slide Transition dialog box.

✦ **Slide Transition Effects menu:** Opens a menu of slide transitions. These transitions define how, during a slide show, one slide leaves the screen and the next slide appears in its place.

✦ **Preset Animation menu:** Opens a menu of text-animation options. These animations define how, during a slide show, lines of body text appear on a slide. This menu provides a complete selection of text animation options, but applies to text only — not other objects on the slide.

✦ **Animation Preview button:** Plays all animation effects applied to the currently selected slide only, so that you can preview how they will look during the actual presentation. The effects play in the small frame where the currently selected slide resides in the Slide Sorter window.

✦ **Hide Slide button:** Toggles to hide/show a slide during a slide show. The Hide Slide function is useful when you want to customize a show by displaying only a subset of slides in the presentation. Slides that you don't want to show can be hidden — but they aren't deleted.

✦ **Rehearse Timings button:** Activates the slide show with a Rehearsal dialog box. If you're running a slide show in stand-alone mode — like at an information kiosk — PowerPoint can advance the slides, in sequence, at any time interval you choose. Rehearse Timings lets you set display durations for each slide.

✦ **Summary Slide button:** Automatically creates a summary slide from slide titles. This new slide is titled Summary Slide and consists of a list of bullets, with each bullet showing the title of a slide in the presentation. If the presentation is very long — too long to list all the title bullets on a single Summary Slide — the Summary Slide extends into two or three Summary Slides to accommodate a listing of all slide titles. Spillover Summary Slides are titled Summary Slide (cont.). Format Summary Slides using the design of the Slide Master.

✦ **Speaker Notes button:** Displays the Speaker Notes dialog box so that you can add or edit speaker notes for the current slide. The text you add or edit in this dialog box is identical to the text that appears in the Notes pane of the Normal view for the current slide.

✦ **Common Tasks:** Displays the Common Tasks menu, which includes the New Slide button, Slide Layout button, and Apply Design Template button.

 Another button that you may find useful when working in Slide Sorter view is the Show Formatting button, located on the Standard toolbar. Show Formatting toggles between showing complete slide layouts (text, color, and graphics) or hiding everything except unformatted slide titles. (In Normal view and Outline view, the Show Formatting button toggles between showing formatted and unformatted text in the Outline pane.) Hiding slide layouts allows you to save time when you're working in Slide Sorter view. Every time you make a change to your slides in Slide Sorter view — such as reordering slides — PowerPoint must redraw your slide miniatures to reflect the changes made. It takes more time for PowerPoint to draw the slide miniatures when it shows formatting than to simply draw black and white slide miniatures with the titles only.

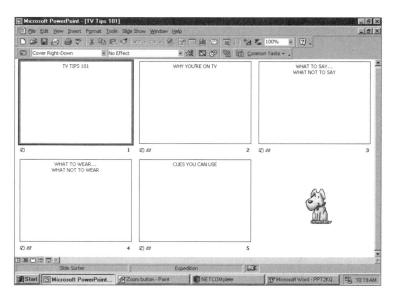

Return to Normal view or Slide view at any time by double-clicking
any slide in Slide Sorter view. The view that you return to is the
view you were in prior to clicking the Slide Sorter view button.

Moving slides around

Moving and reordering slides is a snap when you're working in
Slide Sorter view. Just follow these steps to shuffle your slides
around:

1. Click the slide that you want to move.

To move multiple slides as a group, hold down the Shift key as
you click each slide that you want included in the group.

2. Click and hold the mouse button to drag the slide (or slide
group) to position it between two other slides in the stack. A
long, blinking cursor symbol indicates where the slide (or
slide group) will be repositioned.

3. Release the mouse button. The slide or slides are repositioned,
and the entire stack of slides is renumbered accordingly.

Adding and duplicating slides

To add a new slide:

1. In Slide Sorter view, click between the two slides where you
want to insert the new slide. The long, blinking cursor marks
the spot for insertion.

2. Click the New Slide button or press Ctrl+M and choose an
AutoLayout for the new slide. The new slide is added where
you positioned the cursor.

To add a slide from another presentation:

1. n Slide Sorter view, click between the two slides where you
want to insert the slide from another presentation. The long,
blinking cursor marks the spot for insertion.

2. Switch to the other presentation by clicking on the other
presentation's window, and move to the Slide Sorter view.

3. Click the slide that you want to copy and add to your original
presentation.

4. Copy the selected slide by selecting Edit⊏>Copy from the Menu
bar or pressing Ctrl+C.

5. Return to your original presentation by clicking its presenta-tion window and choosing Edit➪Paste from the Menu bar or pressing Ctrl+V. The slide is added to your original presenta-tion at the point of insertion. The inserted slide picks up the formatting of the presentation that it is inserted into.

Duplicating a slide is a quick way of copying and pasting a slide in a single step. To duplicate a slide:

1. In Slide Sorter view, click the slide that you want to clone.

2. Choose Edit➪Duplicate from the Menu bar. The duplicate slide is inserted immediately after the original slide.

See also "Moving slides around" earlier in this section for details on moving the position of your added or duplicated slides.

Deleting slides

Keep these tips in mind when you want to chuck a slide from your presentation while using Slide Sorter view:

✦ To delete a slide, click the slide and press Backspace or Delete.

✦ To delete multiple slides, hold down the Shift key as you click each slide that you want to delete; then press Backspace or Delete to delete the entire group.

✦ To retrieve a deleted slide, choose Edit➪Undo Delete Slide from the Menu bar.

The slide stack is renumbered accordingly.

Working with Templates and Masters

The fastest, most effective way to put together an attractive, professional-looking PowerPoint presentation is to take advantage of templates and customize them to suit your needs.

The PowerPoint templates provide preformatted, professionally designed backgrounds, images, and text colors that make readable, eye-catching slides. Some of the templates also provide content or offer preset animation.

You can make adjustments to the template that change all your slides at one time by editing the Slide Master. As you construct each slide, you can override the Master and make necessary changes to each slide individually. I tell you how to do all this, and more, in this part.

In this part . . .

- ✔ Selecting a template
- ✔ Creating your own template
- ✔ Setting up Master formats
- ✔ Using headers and footers
- ✔ Modifying slide backgrounds
- ✔ Setting up the Title Slide
- ✔ Making adjustments to individual slides

Applying and Creating Templates

PowerPoint comes stocked with tons of premade *templates* — artistic blueprints for constructing your slide presentations quickly and easily. Templates are set up with predefined formatting settings (color schemes, graphic elements, and styled fonts) to minimize the time and effort that you spend building slides.

After applying a template, you can tweak it for an individual presentation by modifying the Slide Master and the Title Master. If you find that you keep making the same adjustments over and over again, you can also create and save your own template.

Applying a template to a new presentation

If you are just starting a new presentation, and you want the slides to follow a template, just follow these steps:

1. Click the Template option in the PowerPoint dialog box that appears when you first open PowerPoint.

2. In the New Presentation dialog box that appears, choose and click a template from one of the following tabs:

- **General tab:** Contains a Blank Presentation template and the AutoContent Wizard template. A Blank Presentation means you'll be working with a template of black text on a white background with no artistic design elements. You can either leave this template as is (a good option if you plan to print your presentation as black and white overhead transparencies) or embellish the template with your own colors and design elements. *See also* Part II for more information on working with the AutoContent Wizard.

- **Design Templates tab:** Contains 44 ready-to-go templates without content. The styles differ from those in the Presentation folder, and the designs are just gorgeous. Check out Ribbons and Romanesque.

- **Presentations tab:** Contains 24 content-inclusive templates, such as Communicating Bad News or Motivating A Team. Most of these templates use different colors and layouts. The content text provides suggested talking points for the template you selected. You can use the content or dump it by deleting the text on each slide and typing in your own information.

- **Office 97 Templates:** Contains 53 templates that may be near and dear to you if you previously used PowerPoint 97. *Note:* This tab exists only if you previously installed PowerPoint 97.

Click a template once to check out a thumbnail sketch of it.

3. Click OK to apply the template. If you chose a Design Template or a template from a previous version of Office, the New Slide dialog box now appears. If you chose a Presentation template, a multi-slide presentation of the type you selected now appears in Normal view.

4. If you're presented with the New Slide dialog box, PowerPoint asks you to choose an AutoLayout for your first slide. Click an AutoLayout and click OK. AutoLayouts provide options for arranging information on your slide. For example, one AutoLayout provides an area for typing title text at the top of the slide and another area for typing bulleted items of text below the title. Another AutoLayout provides an area for typing title text and an organization chart. You can choose from 24 AutoLayouts, including a Blank AutoLayout that lets you add whatever types of text or objects you want to the slide.

If you want to tweak the template a bit to suit your own purposes and preferences, *see also* "Editing the Slide Master" later in this part for details on how to do so.

Applying a template to an existing presentation

You can easily change templates at any point while creating your presentation. However, before you do so, you need to be aware of the following things:

✦ The template is applied to all slides in the entire presentation. PowerPoint doesn't allow a mix-and-match approach, so you can't use one template for a few slides and another template for a few others.

✦ Applying a new template obliterates any modifications that you made to the Slide Master for the previously used template. Applying a new template copies the template's background colors, text formatting, decorations — everything — onto your Masters and all slides throughout the presentation.

✦ Changes made to the colors and formatting of non-Master items on individual slides, though, aren't affected by the application of the new template. Any custom-tailoring of non-Master elements on individual slides (except background color) remains safe, as PowerPoint preserves such deviations regardless of changes in the Master. For example, if you add a clip art to a particular slide, the clip art is still there after you apply a new template.

To apply a template to an existing presentation, just follow these steps:

1. Open the presentation and choose Format⇨Apply Design Template from the Menu bar; or choose Apply Design Template from the Common Tasks drop-down list on the Formatting toolbar or Slide Sorter toolbar. You can also double-click the name of the template in the status bar at the bottom of the PowerPoint window. The Apply Design Template dialog box appears, and you can search through its folders to select a template.

2. Choose and click a template from one of these locations in the Apply Design Template dialog box:

- **Presentation Designs folder:** Contains 44 ready-to-go templates without content — the same stuff you find under Design Templates in the New Presentation dialog box.

- **1033 folder:** Contains 24 content-inclusive templates — the same templates located under the Presentations tab in the New Presentation dialog box.

3. Click Apply. You now see the new template applied to your slides. If you want to tweak the template, *see also* "Editing the Slide Master" later in this part for details.

In the event that you get tired of using the templates that shipped with PowerPoint 2000, you can obtain fresh new ones just by going online. Get the latest templates by choosing Help➪Office on the Web from the Menu bar to connect to the Office Update Web site. At the Office Update Site, choose PowerPoint to obtain menus leading to additional templates that you can download and use.

Creating an original template

Don't like any of PowerPoint's templates? Create your own! A template is basically just a set of style elements for your slides, so creating your own is easy. You can create a new template at any time, and save it into the templates folder for application to existing or new presentations. Saving a template is almost identical to saving a presentation — except that the template has no slides, but only Masters. You save a template with a different PowerPoint file extension, too.

Just follow these steps to create a new template:

1. From anywhere within PowerPoint, choose File➪New.

2. Select any template from the New Presentation dialog box — you're modifying it to suit your needs anyway.

You may want to select a template that most closely resembles the new template that you want to create. Doing so helps reduce the amount of tweaking you have to do to the template. Choosing a Blank template lets you design everything from scratch.

3. Click Cancel in the Add New Slide dialog box.

4. Modify the template by choosing View➪Master from the Menu bar and then choosing any or all Masters that you want to change. You may wish to format text fonts and point sizes, adjust the background color, or add thematic pictures or logos to each Master. (*See also* "Editing the Slide Master" later in this part.)

5. Save your newly created template by choosing File➪Save from the Menu bar.

Store your new template in the same folder as the other PowerPoint templates so that you know where to look when trying to retrieve it. Your PowerPoint templates are probably stored in Program Files⇨Microsoft Office⇨Templates. Choose a subfolder within Templates, or create a new one for your own special creations.

The typical PowerPoint template extension is POT. If you create a new template titled "Wacky," save it by the name, Wacky.POT in the templates folder. Under Save as Type, choose Presentation Template.

The next time you peruse template choices in the Apply Design Template dialog box, you'll see your newly created template appear among the template options.

Editing the Handout Master

The Handout Master allows you to lay out the appearance of your presentation as a hard copy audience handout. You have the following two options for your handouts:

✦ **The presentation outline:** Your handouts show only a collapsed outline of your presentation material.

✦ **Small versions of the presentation slides:** This option shows the full text of your handouts in miniature. You can choose how many slide images appear on the printed page. You have the option of 2, 3, 4, 6, or 9 slides per page.

You also have the option of adding placeholders on the Handout Master for the following items:

✦ **Headers and footers:** Headers are placed at the top of the handouts, and footers are placed at the bottom. You can click the placeholder for any header or footer to change the font, format, and content of the text contained within that placeholder.

✦ **Date or page number:** These fields are automatically updated.

To format the Handout Master for your presentation, follow these steps:

1. From any view, choose View⇨Master⇨Handout Master. The Handout Master appears.

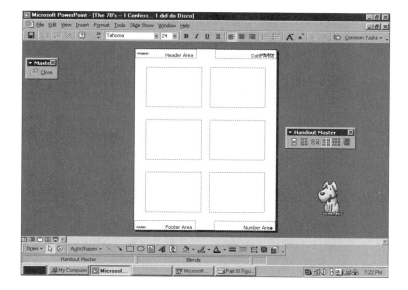

2. Right-click the mouse to open the Handout Master Layout dialog box.

3. At the Handout Master Layout dialog box, click the selection box for all the placeholders that you want located on the Master. Placeholders already in use are deselected and show check marks in their check boxes. Click OK to close the Handout Master Layout dialog box.

4. At the Handout Master toolbox, click whether you want 2, 3, 4, 6, or 9 slides per page, or the presentation outline shown on the handouts. The Handout Master generates dashed outlines showing where the slides or outline are printed. (If you inadvertently close the Handout Master toolbar or it doesn't otherwise appear on-screen, you can make it rematerialize by choosing View⇨Toolbars⇨Handout Master.)

When you're finished formatting the Handout Master, click any view button to return to your presentation. You may want to print and peruse your handouts by choosing File⇨Print from the Menu bar.

Editing the Notes Master

Notes pages are printed pages that you — the speaker — create to remind yourself what you want to say about each slide during your presentation. You can add notes to every slide in your presentation, or only to those slides where you want to provide reminders for yourself. Notes pages are also referred to as Speaker Notes, and are typically used only by the speaker giving the PowerPoint presentation — not for distribution to participating audiences.

Notes can be added to a slide by typing in the notes pane of a slide in Normal view. (*See also* Part I for additional details on working in Normal view.) To add notes in Slide Sorter view, you click the slide where you want to add notes, press the Speaker Notes button on the Slide Sorter toolbar, and type your text in the Speaker Notes dialog box that appears.

A printed Notes page typically appears as a slide thumbnail at the top of the page, followed by a text block consisting of your typed notes. The Notes Master dictates how your presentation's speaker notes appear in hard copy form. It serves as a handy guide for laying out the position and relative size of the slide thumbnail, speaker note text, and other information that you may want to include on your notes.

The Notes Master gives you the option of adding placeholders to reserve places on each notes page for special information. You can add placeholders for the following:

✦ **Slide image:** Places a slide thumbnail on the Notes page. After you add a slide image to the Notes Master, it can be resized by clicking its placeholder and adjusting the sizing handles. The slide image can also be moved by clicking and dragging the placeholder to a new location on the Notes page.

✦ **Notes Body Area:** Reserves an area where you can type your speaker notes. After you add notes to the Notes Master, the Notes Body area can be resized by clicking its placeholder and adjusting the sizing handles.

✦ **Date Area:** Automatically places the current date and time on each of your Notes pages. The Date Area can be moved by clicking and dragging its placeholder to a new location on the Notes page.

✦ **Header:** Reserves a small zone for placing text at the top of each notes page.

✦ **Footer:** Reserves a zone for placing text at the bottom of each notes page.

✦ **Number Area:** Reserves a zone for inserting the page number at the bottom of each notes page.

After you decide which placeholders you want on your speaker notes, follow these steps to format the Notes Master:

1. From any view, choose <u>V</u>iew⇨<u>M</u>aster⇨<u>N</u>otes Master from the Menu bar to call up the Notes Master.

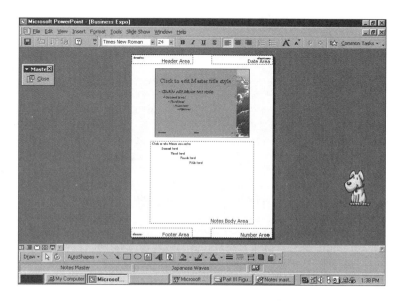

2. Right-click the mouse to open the Notes Master <u>L</u>ayout dialog box.

3. At the Notes Master Layout dialog box, click the selection box of each placeholder that you want located on the Master. Placeholders already in use are deselected. Click OK to close the Notes Master Layout dialog box.

After adding any placeholder, you can click the placeholder and drag it anywhere on the Notes Master page to reposition it. You can also resize each placeholder by clicking and dragging any of its sizing handles. You can also click any text placeholder and edit the font, format, and content of the text contained within that placeholder. If you choose to add date or page number placeholders to the Notes Master, these fields are automatically updated.

4. When you finish formatting the Notes Master, click any view button to return to your presentation. Regardless of when you format the Notes Master, you can add notes to any slide in your presentation at any time. Printed Notes pages follow the formatting you set up on the Notes Master. *See also* Part VIII for specific information about adding speaker notes to individual slides.

Editing the Slide Master

After applying a template, you can make adjustments to it by fiddling with your presentation's Slide Master, which controls all aspects of how slides are constructed: background color; font, size, and color of the text; display of any decorations, borders, or logos; and position of all elements on the slide. If you're creating an original template, you spend lots of time with the Slide Master.

With the exception of the title slide, every slide in your presentation uses the Slide Master format as a layout (unless you specify otherwise). Changing the Slide Master alters every slide in the presentation — adding a polka-dot border to the Master adds a polka-dot border to each and every one of your slides.

Regardless of which fancy colors or decorative elements appear on the Slide Master, every Slide Master contains two text placeholders called the Title Area for AutoLayouts and the Object Area for AutoLayouts. The Title Area for AutoLayouts prescribes how the formatting of slide titles looks, and the Object Area for AutoLayouts prescribes how the formatting of bulleted slide text looks. Any text formatting you apply to these Slide Master text placeholders is applied to text boxes in the same position on slides in the presentation.

If you type specific text in the Title Area or Object Area placeholders, the text doesn't appear on your slides. Placeholder text is shown only as an example of the formatting and placement of text on your slides.

You can create text items that recur on all slides, but not by using the Title Area or Object Area placeholders.

The following list shows you how to modify the Slide Master:

1. Choose View⇨Master⇨Slide Master from the Menu bar, or press Shift and click the Slide View button to bring up the Slide Master.

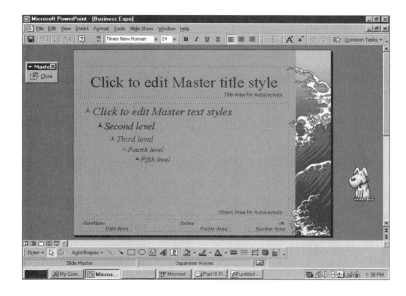

2. Edit the Slide Master as you like. (*See also* Part IV for details about formatting text, and Part V for extensive details on adding and editing multimedia elements.)

PowerPoint applies text formatting changes to entire paragraphs in the Master — just click anywhere within the paragraph, and your formatting changes apply to the whole shmear. This text formatting on the Master is applied to all paragraphs in the same position on slides throughout your presentation.

The Master text styles in the body object have five different preset levels of indentation. You can change how the text and bullets are formatted on each level independently of every other level. For example, you can make first-level bullets appear as check marks, and all lower-level bullets appear as small boxes. Any slide you later create with an AutoLayout that includes bullets follows the Master text bullet formatting you establish.

3. Choose View⇨Normal or click the Normal View button to close the Slide Master and return to Normal view.

Voilà! Your slides magically morph according to the changes made on the Slide Master.

If the text boxes on your Slide Master are bumping into other Master items (such as clip art), just click each text box and reposition it by dragging it to a new location.

Another option is to resize a text box by selecting it (with a single click), and then adjust one of the *handles* that mark the edges of the box. You know you can select a handle when your regular cursor arrow converts to a small double-tipped arrow. After selecting a handle, the double-tipped arrow converts to a small cross (and stays that way) as you resize the box. Adjust the handle by clicking and dragging it to shrink or stretch the text box. To maintain the proportions of a text box, hold the shift key down during resizing. (By the way, resizing via the object handles applies not just to text boxes, but to all other objects you add to the Master.)

Inserting headers and footers

PowerPoint gives you an easy method of applying several finishing touches to your presentation in the footer of each slide. The program also allows you to add both headers and footers to notes and handout pages.

Footers are automatically placed at the bottom of a PowerPoint slide or page, and headers are placed at the top. Regardless of their initial positions, however, you can reposition their placement to best suit your needs. Here's how to insert headers and footers:

1. From any view, choose View⇨Header and Footer from the Menu bar to bring up the Header and Footer dialog box.

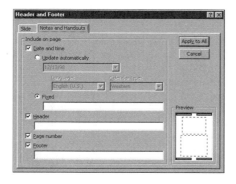

2. Click either the Slide tab or the Notes and Handouts tab. After working on one tab, you can click the remaining tab to work on it.

3. Fill in any of the following boxes:

- **Date and time:** Displays the date and time. You can choose Update automatically or Fixed. Using Fixed means that whatever date and time you type is used, regardless of what day you actually give the presentation.

- **Slide number (Slide tab only):** Displays the slide number.

- **Page number (Notes and Handouts tab only):** Displays the page number.

- **Header (Notes and Handouts tab only):** Displays any recurring text that you want to place at the top of your notes and handouts.

- **Footer:** Displays any other recurring text that you want to place on your slides or notes and handouts.

4. Click Apply to all to make the changes take effect throughout your presentation.

 On the Slide tab, you can click the check box for Don't show on title slide, so that the changes take effect on every slide except the title slide. On the Slide tab you can also click Apply (instead of Apply to all) to make the changes applicable to the current slide only.

 You can reposition headers and footers anywhere on the slides by switching to the Slide Master and then dragging the placeholders to new locations.

You can also edit the header and footer placeholders directly by displaying the Master, clicking each placeholder, and typing in your information.

Picking master color schemes

PowerPoint offers incredibly flexible options for tinting your slides. You can fuss with minute details of coloring the masters, but letting PowerPoint serve as your personal designer is a whole lot easier. You can even choose a different color scheme for each master.

Here's how to use one of the well-coordinated, visually appealing color schemes that PowerPoint offers you (and how to adjust the colors to your liking, if you're the persnickety type):

 1. Choose View⇨Master from the Menu bar and select the master on which you wish to change the color scheme.

2. Choose Format➪Color Scheme to bring up the Color Scheme dialog box for the selected master.

3. Choose an option:

- **To pick a PowerPoint color scheme:** Click the Standard tab and double-click a scheme that you like. You can also single-click a scheme and then click Preview to decide whether you really want to apply the scheme.

- **To change the colors of individual scheme elements:** Click the Custom tab, double-click any element in the Color Scheme dialog box, and choose a new color.

4. Click Apply to use the new scheme only on the current slide, notes page, or handout page; or click Apply to all to change all slides, notes pages, or handouts in your entire presentation.

Even if you choose to use a dark color scheme for slides, consider using a coordinated light color scheme for notes pages and hand-outs . . . you can economize on printer ink cartridges that way.

Shading background colors

You can also change the shading of a slide's background color to obtain a richer feel than you achieve with just plain old brown or plain old orange. To alter background shading

1. From any view except Slide Show view, choose Format➪ Background from the Menu bar. This opens the Background dialog box.

2. Click the color drop-down menu (in the lower portion of the Background fill area) and select Fill Effects. This opens the Fill Effects dialog box.

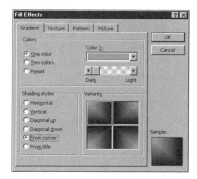

3. Click the Gradient tab and click one or two colors, along with a Shading style. The Shading style allows you to choose how your selected colors blend together on the slide backgrounds: horizontally, vertically, or in some other combination.

The Fill Effects dialog box also has Texture, Pattern, and Picture tabs.

- **Texture:** I definitely recommend trying out several of the textures as backgrounds — some of them are absolutely beautiful!

- **Pattern:** As a general rule, you should stay away from using patterns on the background; they make text extremely hard to read.

- **Picture:** Be cautious about using imported pictures, which can also create readability problems. Use background pictures only when they don't compete with text that appears on top of the picture.

As you tinker with assorted selections, click the Preview button at any time to check out your chosen backgrounds.

It's easy to go overboard when tinkering with colors. In order to make your presentation as readable as possible, keep the following tips in mind:

✦ Steer clear of bright red backgrounds and avoid busy patterns (checkerboard, thin stripes, Scottish plaid, and so on). These extremes usually don't display well, especially when you're routing slide presentations via the computer.

✦ Midnight blue, dark green, and purple make beautiful, professional-looking backgrounds, particularly when paired with white or yellow text.

✦ Shaded backgrounds look great when blending colors of similar intensities. For example, black and the darkest shade of magenta blend well; beige and pastel yellow blend well; and aqua and spring green blend to create an ocean feel.

✦ Use white as the primary background color when making transparencies and handouts.

✦ Use a color other than white as the primary background color when making on-screen graphics, 35mm slides, and Web-based presentations.

Deleting Master components

Deleting an object on the Slide Master is a snap:

1. Retrieve the Slide Master by choosing View➪Master➪Slide Master from the menu bar or press Shift and click the Slide View button.

2. Click the object that you want to delete. To wipe out an entire text object, first click anywhere on the text; then click again on the object frame.

3. Press the Backspace or Delete key, choose Edit➪Cut, or click the Cut button on the Standard toolbar.

If you erroneously delete an object, just undo your mistake by choosing Edit➪Undo from the Menu bar, or by clicking the Undo button on the Standard toolbar.

You can't move or edit Slide Master elements from the slides themselves. I wasted plenty of time trying to delete a theme picture on Slide #7 only to realize (after much frustration) that I can't grab the darn thing because it's not on the slide — it's on the Slide Master.

Editing the Title Master

I usually start off each PowerPoint presentation with a slide that shows the title of my presentation along with a subtitle showing my name. I suppose many other presenters do the same thing, and that's why PowerPoint offers you a handy way to create a special first slide — a Title Slide — for your presentation.

You can add a Title slide to your presentation by switching to Slide Sorter view and adding a new slide to the left of Slide #1. Choose the Title Slide AutoLayout in the New Slide dialog box.

PowerPoint provides you with a separate Title Master for designing title slides. The idea is that you can use it to format your title slide differently than the rest of your slide presentation. The Title Master also has slightly different design elements than the Slide Master to give it a unique look — but one that coordinates well with the rest of the presentation.

Call up the Title Master as follows:

1. In Slide view or Normal view, move to the first slide in your presentation (assuming that the first slide is the title slide).

2. Choose View⇨Master⇨Title Master. The Title Master appears.

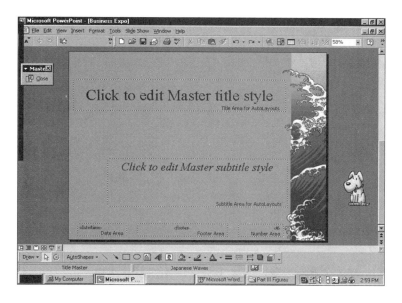

3. Alter the Title Master to your heart's content. *See also* "Editing the Slide Master" earlier in this part for additional details.

The Title Master differs from — but coordinates nicely with — the Slide Master for a given template. Note, however, that the Object Area for AutoLayouts is replaced with the Subtitle Area for AutoLayouts. The only difference this makes is that less room is reserved in the lower half of the Title Slide for placing text. Remember, though, that you can always resize — or even delete — a text box to meet your own specific requirements.

4. Click the Slide View or Normal View button to return to your first slide — your Title Slide — and examine how it looks.

Overriding the Master Style on a Single Slide

Using masters is optional, but just as you wouldn't build a house without a floor plan, you don't want to build a PowerPoint presentation without masters. Why waste time performing the same ten formatting steps on each of 20 slides when you can format them once on the master and be done with it?

You can, however, disregard the master format for a particular slide, which allows you to modify individual slides as needed without altering the rest of your presentation. The processes of adding and moving text and objects on an individual slide are the same as those you use to alter the master slides.

Changing the text formatting

Suppose you created nine slides that lead to a critical, culminating key point, and to ensure that every participant's brain captures and processes this super-important key point, you want to use bright gold, italic, 60-point Impact — but just on this one slide.

Use the following steps to make changes to the Master style of text on one particular slide:

1. Move to the slide where you want to make the change.

2. Switch to Normal view or Slide view.

 3. Click the text box and select (highlight) the text that you want to edit. Use the Formatting toolbar to make your changes. The changes don't alter the Slide Master; they apply to this individual slide only.

Changing the background color

If you want to change the background color on a single slide, just follow these steps:

1. In any view, move to the slide where you want to use a different background.

2. Choose Format⇨Background to bring up the Background dialog box.

3. Click the color drop-down arrow to reveal a menu for changing the background color to your preference. *See also* "Shading background colors" earlier in this part.

4. Click the Apply button to make the changes on the current slide.

Do *not* click the Apply to all button, or every slide in your presentation is affected.

Clicking the Apply to all button at this stage is a convenient way of editing the Slide Master without opening up the Master itself.

Deleting background objects

To obliterate the master objects from a given slide, follow these steps:

1. In Slide view or Normal view, move to the slide where you want to delete background objects.

2. Choose Format⇨Background to bring up the Background dialog box.

3. Click the Omit background graphics from master check box so that a check mark appears in the box.

4. Click Apply. Master objects immediately disappear from the current slide.

Reverting to the master style

If you don't like the changes you made to an individual slide, you can choose Edit⇨Undo to undo your most recent change. Or if you want to reapply the Slide Master style to the entire slide, here's what you do:

1. Switch to any view except Slide Show view.

2. Choose Format⇨Slide Layout to bring up the Slide Layout dialog box.

3. Click the Reapply button to restore all formatting specified by the Slide Master.

To change more than one slide back to the master style, switch to Slide Sorter view, press Shift, click each slide that you want to revert to your master style, and then follow Steps 2 and 3.

Part IV

Adding Text

The single most important element you place on your slides is text. After all, the text is what conveys the essence of your presentation — the key points that you want your audience to remember. This part shows you how to present that text in the most effective way.

In this part . . .

- ✔ **Working with text boxes**
- ✔ **Aligning blocks of text**
- ✔ **Aligning text with indents and tabs**
- ✔ **Adding bullets**
- ✔ **Quickly changing capitalization**
- ✔ **Cutting, copying, and pasting text**
- ✔ **Finding and replacing text**
- ✔ **Modifying the appearance of your text**
- ✔ **Checking your spelling**
- ✔ **Undoing errors**

About Text Boxes

All slides — the Slide Master, the Title Master, and all slide AutoLayouts except the Blank slide option — appear with at least one *text box* (a zone reserved for adding text).

You need to know the following about text boxes:

✦ You can enlarge or shrink a text box, but you can't change its shape — text boxes are always rectangular.

✦ Text boxes are marked by lightly dashed lines. You type inside the boundaries of each box, although your typed text may not actually fill up the entire box.

✦ You can move text boxes around on the slide, which is useful when a text box bumps into another slide element, such as clip art.

✦ You can delete text boxes and add new ones, as needed.

Adding text boxes

You can add as many text boxes to a slide as you like. Each text box can be formatted and moved independently from all the other text boxes. To add a text box, just follow these steps:

1. In Slide view or Normal view, click the Text Box button on the Drawing toolbar.

2. Point the I-beam cursor to the position on your slide where you want the upper-left corner of your new text box.

3. Click and hold the mouse as you drag the cursor to position the lower-right corner of your new text box. The cursor appears as a crosshair during the positioning, and you see solid edges appear as the borders of the box.

4. Release the mouse button after you give the text box the desired proportions.

The new text box is now complete. Click inside the box to type text, or click the edge of the box to format how text appears inside the box.

Selecting text boxes

Before you can modify a text box, you have to identify for PowerPoint which text box you want to work on. To select a text box:

1. In Slide view or Normal view, click the Select Objects button on the Drawing toolbar.

2. Point the arrow anywhere along the border of the text box that you want to edit; then click the left mouse button. The text box suddenly sprouts *handles* — dots marking the corners and sides of the box. The appearance of handles indicates that the text box is selected.

Resizing or moving text boxes

After you select a text box, you're free to resize and move the box as you want. Go wild! And follow these simple guidelines along the way:

✦ **To move a text box:** Click and hold down the mouse button anywhere along the edge of the text box — except on a handle! Drag the box anywhere on the slide and release the mouse button.

✦ **To change the size of a text box while keeping the original proportions:** Click and hold down the mouse button on any of the corner handles, drag the handle to enlarge or shrink the text box proportionally, and then release the mouse button. To keep the center of the box positioned in the same spot during resizing, hold down the Ctrl key while dragging a sizing handle.

✦ **To change the proportions of a text box:** Click and hold down the mouse button on any of the side handles. Drag the top or bottom handle to increase or decrease the text box's height; drag the left or right handle to adjust the width.

Importing text into a text box

You may import text from outside PowerPoint (such as from a word-processing program) for inclusion in a text box. Import text as follows:

1. In your word-processing program, select the text you wish to copy onto the PowerPoint slide.

 2. In your word-processing program, copy the selected text by choosing Edit⇨Copy, clicking the Copy button, or pressing Ctrl+C.

3. In PowerPoint, switch to Slide view or Normal view and click inside the slide where you want to add the copied text.

 4. Paste the selected text by choosing Edit⇨Paste, clicking the Paste button, or pressing Ctrl+V.

Moving around and typing inside a text box

You type and edit text in a PowerPoint text box in virtually the same way that you use a word processor. But first you have to tell PowerPoint that you want to manipulate the text:

 1. Click the Select Objects button on the Drawing toolbar.

2. Click inside the text box. A thick border appears around the text box, a solid background color appears behind the text, and the arrow changes to an I-beam inside the text box — all of which indicate that you can now start typing.

You need to know the following tips about typing and editing in a text box:

✦ **Wrapping words to the next line:** When you reach the end of a line, keep typing — PowerPoint automatically moves to the next line. You press Enter only when you want to begin a new paragraph.

✦ **Using AutoFit text in a text box:** If you attempt to type more text than can fit in your text box, PowerPoint automatically adjusts the point size of the text to fit the box.

✦ **Using the keyboard to navigate through the text:** Use the ↑, ↓, ←, and → keys on your keyboard to move the cursor up or down one line, or left or right one character.

✦ **Using the mouse to navigate through the text:** Move the mouse until the little I-beam is positioned where you want to make an edit and then click the left mouse button. The I-beam cursor instantly repositions itself to your chosen destination.

✦ **Selecting text (marking text to be edited):** Use one of these methods:

• Press the Shift key while simultaneously pressing an arrow key to highlight an entire block of text.

• Use the mouse to point to the beginning of the text that you want to mark; then click and drag the mouse over the text. The text is highlighted as you drag. Release the button when you reach the end of the block.

✦ **Deleting text:** First highlight the text to be deleted and then press the Backspace key or the Delete key to delete the text.

If you change text attributes (formatting, aligning, and so on) without first marking a block of text, the changes kick in at the cursor location. In other words, you see the text change that you indicated as soon as you start typing. Repositioning the cursor to another location, however, doesn't carry with it the text formatting you've established.

Aligning Paragraphs of Text

Adjust the way your text lines up by selecting an entire text box or selecting only specific lines of text within a text box. Then choose Format⇨Alignment from the Menu bar or click the appropriate toolbar button to align your selected text. PowerPoint provides you with several ways to align text on your slides:

✦ **Centered:** Multiple slides on the same topic can have the title centered on the first slide and deleted altogether on all subsequent, related slides. Short, unbulleted text items also look nice centered, because differences in the length of each line help effectively distinguish line items.

✦ **Left-aligned:** For bulleted body text and short sentences, use left alignment, which lines up text neatly against the left edge of the text box.

✦ **Right-aligned:** For something different, try right alignment, which lines up text neatly down the right side of the text box.

✦ **Justified:** Justified text alignment centers text in the box and also lines up each edge of the text. This alignment looks good for formatting a paragraph of narrative text — such as an excerpt from a speech — on your slide.

Aligning Text with Indents and Tabs

Each individual text box has its own ruler for measuring the length of the box and for setting the location of indents and tabs within the box. A separate ruler exists for each text box on a slide. Settings you define for this ruler affect all text within the box. You can establish different settings for different text boxes, but not for individual lines of text within a box.

To align text by setting indents and tabs:

1. Turn on the ruler by choosing View➪Ruler from the Menu bar.

2. Click inside the text box in which you wish to set indents and tabs.

3. Click and drag the upper margin setting to define the indent position for new paragraphs within the text box. The upper margin setting appears at the top of the ruler and looks like a small arrow pointing down.

4. Click and drag the lower margin setting to define the indent position for paragraph bodies within the text box. The lower margin setting appears at the bottom of the ruler and looks like a small arrow pointing up.

 5. Click the Tab button repeatedly to select a tab type. Each time you click the Tab button, the tab type changes. Then click a ruler position to add the tab to the ruler.

Bulleting Text

A bullet marks the start of a line to indicate a new text item. Bullets come in many styles, including spots, check marks, and arrows — but they're almost never shaped like real-life bullets.

Follow these steps to bullet your text in PowerPoint:

1. Select the lines or paragraphs of text that you want to bullet. Each bullet must be separated by a paragraph return. For example, if you want a bulleted list of three text items, make sure those three items are separated by paragraph returns.

 2. Click the Bullets button.

The Bullets button operates like an on/off switch (a toggle). Following these steps adds bullets to unbulleted text; repeating the steps removes the bullets.

If you don't like the style of the bullets that appear on-screen, choose Format⇨Bullets and Numbering from the Menu bar to call up the Bullets and Numbering dialog box. In the Bullets and Numbering dialog box, you can select a default bullet character and adjust its font, size, and color. (Clicking None "unbullets" the bulleted text.)

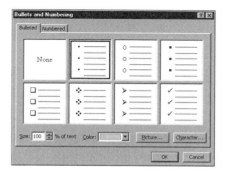

You can also choose a different bullet character by clicking Character in the Bullets and Numbering dialog box to bring up the Bullet dialog box, where you can shop from hundreds of bullet choices for each font.

For those of you who want to get really fancy, clicking Picture in the Bullets and Numbering dialog box allows you to use graphical images as bullets. Clicking Picture brings up the Picture Bullet dialog box — a subset of the Clip Gallery — if you have the Clip Gallery installed. The Picture Bullet dialog box gives you more than 150 bullet choices.

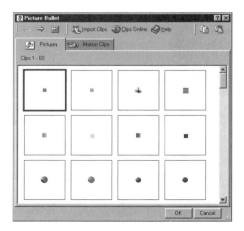

If you haven't installed the Clip Gallery, clicking Picture brings up the Insert Picture dialog box, from which you can select any available picture file to use as a bullet. *See also* Part V for more information on working with pictures and clip art.

 I recommend setting bullet attributes on the Slide Master in order to save time constructing your individual slides. *See also* Part III on adding elements to the Slide Master.

Cutting, Copying, and Pasting Text

PowerPoint uses the same standard Cut, Copy, and Paste commands that are forever present in all Windows-based programs. All three editing commands can be applied to any highlighted text.

Use the following steps when working with the Cut, Copy, and Paste commands:

 ✦ **To copy text:** Select the text that you want to copy and click the Copy button, press Ctrl+C, or choose Edit⇨Copy. Click the cursor wherever you want the text to appear; then paste. The text appears in both locations. You can paste on the same slide or on any other slide in your presentation.

✦ **To duplicate an entire text box:** Click the text box to select it and then choose Edit➪Duplicate. The Duplicate command is disabled when text within a text box is selected. To duplicate selected text within a text box, use Copy and Paste.

 ✦ **To cut and move text:** Select the text that you want to cut and then click the Cut button, press Ctrl+X, or choose Edit➪Cut. Click the cursor wherever you want the text to reappear; then paste. The text appears only in the pasted location. You can paste on the same slide or on any other slide in your presentation.

✦ **To delete text:** Use the Cut command, which allows you to retain your text if you suddenly change your mind (just press Paste). If you're absolutely certain that you want to eradicate certain text forever, select it and choose Edit➪Clear. The Paste command can't bring back cleared text — that text is gone forever unless you immediately choose the Edit➪Undo command.

 ✦ **To paste text:** Click the Paste button, press Ctrl+V, or choose Edit➪Paste.

As in other Windows-based programs, the Cut, Copy, and Paste commands involve the Clipboard. The Office 2000 Clipboard offers many more features than the Windows Clipboard. For example, the Windows Clipboard keeps only the text (or other object) most recently cut or copied; the Office Clipboard can hold as many as 12 items at any given time. Items can be copied and collected from virtually any other program and can remain on the Office Clipboard until you exit all Office programs.

The Office Clipboard is operated with a special Clipboard toolbar that you can bring up by choosing View➪Toolbars➪Clipboard from the Menu bar.

The Clipboard toolbar displays all items currently cut or copied to the Clipboard. Click an item and then click the Copy, Paste, Paste All, or Delete button to manipulate the item. To select multiple items, hold down the Ctrl key as you click each item.

Finding and Replacing Text

The Find and Replace commands are helpful when you need to change one piece of text that appears several times throughout your slides — for example, the date on a series of slides from a long-ago presentation that you want to reuse.

The Find command locates specific words or phrases in your slide stack. Follow these steps to use the Find command:

1. Choose Edit➪Find from the Menu bar or Press Ctrl+F to bring up the Find dialog box.

2. In the Find what area, type the text that you want to locate. If you're looking for an exact match of capital and lowercase letters, click the Match case box. If you want to locate only whole words — not pieces of larger words (like cat in catalog) — click the Find whole words only box.

3. Press Enter to start the search. If you receive a message that the search item wasn't found, that means your search term wasn't located among your slides. Check your spelling and try again.

If your chosen text is located anywhere among your slides, the Find command moves to the first slide containing that text. It also highlights your found text so that you can then edit it or continue searching for the next occurrence.

4. If you want to replace your found text with something else, click the Replace button. A Replace dialog box appears. In the Replace with area, type your replacement text. Then click Replace to replace just the current instance of the found text, or click Replace All to replace every instance of the found text.

5. When you're done finding (or replacing) text, click Close to get rid of the Find dialog box.

If you already know that you want to replace all instances of a given word — like substituting next year's date for this year's date — use the Replace command instead of Find by following these steps:

1. Choose Edit⇨Replace from the Menu bar to call up the Replace dialog box.

2. In the Find what area, type the word or phrase that you want to replace.

3. In the Replace with area, type your replacement text.

4. Click the Replace All button. Every instance of the sought-after text changes to the replacement text.

After replacing text, you may want to check each slide to ensure that the replaced text hasn't messed up the text layout in the text box, which sometimes happens when you replace text of one length with text of a substantially different length.

Formatting Text

The material discussed in this section applies to all PowerPoint text. Procedures for formatting text on the Masters are identical to those used for formatting text on individual slides.

The fastest way to format text for an entire presentation is to format text in the text boxes located on the Slide and Title Masters. Text on all slides in the presentation follows this formatting, eliminating the need for you to format text on a slide-by-slide basis. Individual text boxes on any slide can be reformatted as needed, overriding the formatting prescribed for them by the masters. *See* Part II for more information on working with Masters.

Changing the overall look of text

To adjust the way your text looks (the formatting), highlight the text and then choose one of the following methods:

♦ Open the Font dialog box, which offers one-stop shopping for any and all formatting features, by choosing Format⇨Font from the Menu bar or by clicking the right mouse button and then clicking Font on the shortcut menu.

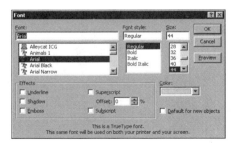

♦ Click a button on the Text Formatting toolbar to change a single formatting feature.

♦ Use a keyboard shortcut to change a formatting feature.

Keyboard Shortcut	Format or Function
Ctrl+B	**Bold**
Ctrl+I	*Italic*
Ctrl+U	Underline
Ctrl+spacebar	Normal (remove formatting)
Ctrl+Shift+F	Font
Ctrl+Shift+P	Highlights the current point size in the Font Size list box on the Standard toolbar. Typing a new number and pressing Enter changes the size of the currently selected text.
Ctrl+Shift+>	Increase point size
Ctrl+Shift+<	Decrease point size

To reset the point size of selected text, click the Font Size area on the Formatting toolbar and type a new point size in the box. You can also click the arrow attached to the Font Size area to reveal a drop-down list of point size choices.

Note: Ctrl+spacebar clears font attributes, such as bold and underline, but it doesn't reset the font or point size of your text.

Changing capitalization for blocks of text

To quickly change the capitalization of text — a single character or a block of text — follow these steps:

1. Highlight the text that you want to capitalize.

2. Choose F<u>o</u>rmat⇨Change Cas<u>e</u> from the Menu bar to bring up
the Change Case dialog box.

3. Choose a capitalization option from the Change Case menu
and click OK.

- **<u>S</u>entence case:** The first letter of the first word in each
sentence is capitalized. All other text is changed to
lowercase.

- **<u>l</u>owercase:** All text is changed to lowercase.

- **<u>U</u>PPERCASE:** All text is changed to uppercase.

- **<u>T</u>itle Case:** The first letter of each word is capitalized
except for articles, such as *a* and *the*.

- **tO<u>G</u>GLE cASE:** Uppercase letters are changed to lowercase
and vice versa. The toggle case option comes in handy
when you discover you've been typing away with the Caps
Lock key on.

Color

Color perks up your text and emphasizes key words and phrases.
If you plan to display your PowerPoint presentation as color
overheads, 35mm slides, computer output, or a Web page, then
invest a little energy in colorizing your text.

 Change the color of highlighted text by clicking the Font Color
button on the Drawing toolbar and clicking a color from the
palette that appears.

If the font colors that pop up don't suffice, click More Font Colors
for even more color choices. If these colors don't meet your needs
either, click the Custom tab and create the one and only perfect
shade that you're searching for by clicking in the spectrum of
<u>C</u>olors and clicking OK.

Embossing

Embossing text adds a dark shadow below the text and a light
shadow above it. Unfortunately, it also changes the distinction
between the text color and the background color, making embossed
text darn near impossible to read. It is nice, however, for creating a

textured background — stamping an embossed company name multiple times on the background of each slide, for example. Background text is very subtle and doesn't interfere with information presented in the text boxes layered in front of the background.

My advice about embossing: Use this function only under very specific conditions. It often complicates your images and makes them very hard to read.

To emboss text, highlight the text; then choose Format⇨Font from the Menu bar and click the Emboss check box. Click OK to apply the changes and close the Font dialog box.

Font

To change the font of highlighted text, click the arrow next to the Font box on the Formatting toolbar and choose a font from the drop-down list that appears.

You can also select a new font in the Font dialog box by choosing Format⇨Font from the Menu bar. Remember to first mark the text that you want to change or to select the text box where the text is located.

PowerPoint places the fonts you use most frequently at the beginning of the font list so that you don't waste time scrolling through the list.

Shadows

Shadowing text adds a touch of class to your slides. It may also improve readability for some slides by making text characters stand out against their PowerPoint background. Apply a shadow to selected text by clicking the Text Shadow button located on the Formatting toolbar.

Size

To change the size of highlighted text, click the Font Size box on the Formatting toolbar; then click a preset point size (sizes range from 8 points to 96 points) or type in the point size you desire.

Best formatting choices

I find the following tips very handy when formatting the text in my presentations:

✦ **Keep color contrast high.** Dark blue or black text works well on light-colored backgrounds. White or yellow text works well on dark backgrounds.

✦ **Keep text point sizes large.** Try to use a text size 32 points or larger, dropping down to 28 points only if you have to. If your information doesn't fit on one slide, break it up into two slides. *Remember:* The purpose of using PowerPoint is to convey information to your audience. If they can't read your slides, you can't succeed! (One exception is to use small fonts for labeling navigation buttons.)

✦ **Avoid using more than two fonts in your presentations.** Think about using one font for titles and another for body text. Use bold, italics, and underlining to set off key information.

✦ **Use simple, easy-to-read fonts on all body text.** For example, basic fonts like Arial are much more readable than frilly ones like Algerian.

✦ **Use fancy fonts sparingly.** Reserve fancy fonts for titles, and use them only when the point size of the title is large enough to maintain the overall clarity of the text.

✦ **Make use of highlighting.** Highlight key words or phrases by marking the important text and using a different color to distinguish it from surrounding text. White or yellow text can be replaced with light green or light orange; black or dark blue text can be replaced by dark magenta or deep teal.

✦ **Keep things simple.** Use shadow text only when it helps improve the readability of your slides. Use bold text often and avoid embossing.

Numbering Lists

PowerPoint offers a quick and easy way to number items in a list, to change numbering styles from Arabic to Roman numbers, and to change numbers to a lettered outline.

Follow these steps to number your text in PowerPoint:

1. Highlight the lines or paragraphs of text that you want to number. Text items must be separated by paragraph returns in order to be given separate numbers.

 2. Click the Numbering button on the Formatting toolbar.

The Numbering button toggles so that clicking it again removes numbering from the text.

To select the type of numbering you want, choose Format⇨Bullets and Numbering from the Menu bar to bring up the Bullets and Numbering dialog box. In the Bullets and Numbering dialog box, select the Numbered tab and choose the size and color of your numbers, and the starting number. (Clicking None removes numbering from the selected text.)

Numbered lists are automatically renumbered when you change the order of items in the list.

Spell-Checking

Correct spelling is vital in everything you communicate to your audience. If you're going to go to the effort of creating crisp, professional slides, you may as well make sure your text is spelled correctly. Besides, nothing is more embarrassing than misspelling a word and displaying your error to a roomful of watchful colleagues. You can check your spelling after you create your slides or while you're in the process of creating them.

PowerPoint can't check grammar — for example, it doesn't flag the word *too* when you really meant to type *to* — and it doesn't check the spelling of embedded objects, like graphs and charts.

After-the-fact

After typing all your text, bring up the spell checker to look for spelling mistakes throughout the document by following these steps:

1. Choose Tools⇨Spelling from the Menu bar or click the Spelling button on the Standard toolbar.

When PowerPoint finds an error, the program shows the faulty slide and highlights the potentially misspelled word. PowerPoint also recommends possible corrections for your error.

2. Accept one of PowerPoint's corrections and click the Change button, click Ignore to leave the word as it is, or type in your own correction.

If PowerPoint red-flags a word that you know is spelled correctly, click Ignore All to have PowerPoint ignore that word throughout the presentation. *See also* "The custom dictionary" later in this part.

If you know that you misspelled a certain word throughout the presentation, click the Change All button and correct all instances of your error in one fell swoop.

For any red-flagged misspelled word, you can type your own correction into the Change to area and press the Change button. This is a useful option when none of the suggested changes are correct spellings for your word.

3. Repeat Steps 1 and 2 until PowerPoint informs you that the spelling check is complete.

On-the-fly

Besides the standard after-the-fact spell checker, PowerPoint also offers an on-the-fly spell checker that verifies the spelling of each word immediately after you type it. The moment you type a word PowerPoint can't understand, it places a wiggly red line under the word in question.

This spell-checking feature is turned on by default. To turn off automatic spell-checking, just follow these steps:

1. Choose Tools➪Options from the Menu bar and click the Spelling and Style tab.

2. In the Spelling area, click to clear the check box for Check spelling as you type.

The custom dictionary

If you use a nonstandard word often, add it to PowerPoint's custom dictionary so that PowerPoint doesn't nag you about it during spell checks (unless you spelled your customized word incorrectly, of course). Whenever PowerPoint incorrectly flags one of your special words, just click the Add words to: custom.dic option. This prevents the word from being considered erroneous in future spell-checks.

Using Multiple Languages

PowerPoint 2000 allows you to create and view presentations in more than 80 languages, and PowerPoint can even support Asian languages and right-to-left text.

The version of PowerPoint sold in the United States automatically detects three of the most frequently used languages — English, Spanish, and French (voilà!) — and comes with proofing tools that automatically know to use the spelling dictionary installed for each language. Foreign date, time, and numbering conventions are also supported for multiple languages.

To make use of PowerPoint's multiple language features, you need to install the MultiLanguage Pack that is located on its own CD and has its own installer. For more information on making use of these features, choose Help⟳Microsoft PowerPoint Help from the Menu bar and type "Microsoft Multilanguage Pack" in the query box.

Undoing Errors

The Undo command is wonderful because it literally undoes your last action. Cleared text reappears. Moved text goes back to its original location. The only thing Undo can't reverse is the passage of time. You can invoke the Undo command in any of three ways:

+ Choose Edit⟳Undo from the Menu bar.

+ Click the Undo button on the Standard toolbar.

+ Press Ctrl+Z.

Undo tracks your 20 most recent actions — but try to fix undo-able errors the minute you notice them. Undo doesn't work on a handful of actions, but PowerPoint typically warns you about this before you execute the action. One such undo-able action is ungrouping certain PowerPoint images into their component objects; this action usually can't be undone (you can't regroup the image into its original composition).

In case you're the finicky sort, PowerPoint also provides a Redo command, which allows you to redo whatever you previously undid. You can use the Redo command as follows:

+ Choose Edit⟳Redo from the Menu bar.

+ Click the Redo button on the Standard toolbar.

+ Press Ctrl+Y.

Part V

Adding Multimedia Goodies

After you get the hang of PowerPoint, mere text and simple backgrounds simply aren't enough to keep you content. Because PowerPoint offers you virtually unlimited multimedia capabilities, you probably want to use them!

Drawing is the quickest and easiest way to add a simple figure or doodle to a PowerPoint slide. The drawing tools let you sketch and colorize basic elements like squares, circles, straight lines, wiggly lines, and any combination of these shapes that you can dream up. For slightly fancier images, you may want to forgo tortured-artist efforts and instead make use of premade images called *clip art.*

And for those among you who strive to Spielberg proportions, PowerPoint makes it easy to incorporate professional photos, movie clips of Aunt Mildred, or sound bites of tapping Riverdancers into your presentation. This part helps you make your presentations play out like symphonies of well-orchestrated graphics, movies, and audio.

In this part . . .

- ✔ Including sounds and movies
- ✔ Adding clip art and photos
- ✔ Drawing lines and shapes
- ✔ Coloring lines and shapes
- ✔ Enhancing images
- ✔ Locating great multimedia goodies
- ✔ Deleting multimedia goodies

About Clips

PowerPoint refers to multimedia goodies — things you put on your slides besides text — as *multimedia clips,* or just *clips.* Clips can include simple drawings, graphic images (clip art and photos), sounds, or movies — all of which serve to enhance the content and quality of your presentation.

PowerPoint provides you with several options for incorporating these clips into your presentation: You can use the Drawing toolbar to draw your own graphics, you can retrieve clips from PowerPoint internal and online libraries known as Clip Galleries, or you can import clips from other external sources.

When using clips imported from programs other than PowerPoint, check the Help section to make certain that PowerPoint supports the file format of your selected clips. If it doesn't, you may need to install new filters from the PowerPoint program CD to accommodate atypical file formats.

About the Drawing Toolbar

Each button or menu on the Drawing toolbar offers a unique tool to assist you in creating something Picasso-esque. You can draw and color simple lines and shapes, and you can shadow and rotate pictures. You can also layer objects in front of (or behind) other objects.

The Drawing toolbar can be used in both Normal and Slide views. Summon the Drawing toolbar by choosing View➪Toolbars➪Drawing from the Menu bar. You can then use the following buttons to create your drawings.

Button	Name
Draw ▾	Draw menu button
▨	Select Objects button
ぴ	Free Rotate button
AutoShapes ▾	AutoShapes menu button
＼	Line button
↘	Arrow button

Button	Name
	Rectangle button
	Oval button
	Text box button
	Insert WordArt button
	Insert Clip Art button
	Fill Color button
	Line Color button
	Font Color button
	Line Style button
	Dash Style button
	Arrow Style button
	Shadow button
	3-D button

Adding Animation

Animation is the term PowerPoint gives to making text and multimedia elements appear on your slides. Rather than having your text and pictures sit lifeless on your slide, you can use animation to create cool effects, like having your text and pictures slowly materialize on the slide.

PowerPoint animation is not as elaborate as *A Bug's Life,* but it's a heck of a lot better than those antique cartoon flip books. (If you've worked with older versions of PowerPoint, you probably remember this process as "building the text" — and that you couldn't animate pictures. Look how far PowerPoint has come!)

You have more than 50 animation effects to choose from, but you should pick one effect per presentation and stick with it. Establishing an easy-to-follow pattern for calling up the next slide and for revealing text and pictures keeps your audience focused on what you're saying rather than how you're saying it.

Animating the slide body

The body of a slide includes text and clip art placed on the slide by an AutoLayout. The body doesn't include the slide title.

Only the parts of your slide prescribed by the slide's AutoLayout will be animated. Added text boxes and other inserted clips won't be animated.

1. Click the Slide Sorter view button in the bottom-left corner of the PowerPoint window to switch to Slide Sorter view. *See also* Part II for more information on working with Slide Sorter view.

2. To apply the same body animation to all slides in your presentation, choose E̲dit⇨Select A̲ll from the Menu bar or press Ctrl+A. If you only want to apply the body animation to a single slide, click the slide where you want to add the animation.

3. Click a body animation effect from the Preset Animation menu on the Slide Sorter toolbar.

There are so many body animation effects to choose from, I suggest you try out a few to get a feel for what looks good — and what doesn't. As soon as you apply an effect to your selected slide, the effect plays on the slide miniature so that you can preview how the effect looks. (If you applied the effect to more than one slide, the preview shows the effect only on the first selected slide.) My favorite effects for body animation are Flys, Peeks, and Zooms.

Avoid using Random Effects because the variation from slide to slide may frustrate your audience.

≡∅ For each slide that you apply body animation to, Slide Sorter view tags the slide with a miniature Animation tag. You can press this tag on any slide to preview how your body animation looks for that slide.

Animating the slide with the Animation Effects toolbar

You can add greater pizzazz and flexibility to your slide's animation by using the Animation Effects toolbar. The Animation Effects toolbar offers some really cool animation effects — most complemented with sounds — to animate the body of your slides.

You can access the Animation Effects toolbar by choosing View⇨Toolbars⇨Animation Effects from the Menu bar.

The following table explains the animation options available on the Animation Effects toolbar.

Choosing This Button	*. . . Does This*
Animate Title	Applies selected animation effect to the title (use in conjunction with an animation option)
Animate Text	Applies selected animation effect to selected text object (use in conjunction with an animation option)
Drive-In Effect	Clip or text flies in from the right, accompanied by an Indianapolis 500 car screech
Flying Effect	Clip or text flies in from the left, accompanied by a Whoosh sound like a flying pizza
Camera Effect	Clip or text shutters open like a camera shutter from its center, accompanied by a camera sound
Flash Once	Clip or text flashes on-screen and then disappears
Laser Text Effect	Text shoots on-screen from upper-right corner, one letter at a time, accompanied by pulsing laser sound
Typewriter Text Effect	Text types on-screen, one letter at a time, accompanied by a typewriter sound
Drop-In Text Effect	Text falls into place from top of screen, one word at a time
Animation Order	Sequences the order in which objects are animated during the slide show. In Slide view, click a slide element (the slide title, a text box or clip). Then type a number in the Animation Order box to tell PowerPoint when that slide element is to be animated. Repeat for each slide element. When that slide appears during a Slide Show, the slide element given the number 1 is animated first. The slide element given the number 2 is animated next, and so on.
Custom Animation	Opens the Custom Animation dialog box (see the following section for more information)

Animate your slide using the Animation Effects toolbar by following these steps:

1. Select the parts of the slide that you want to animate. To animate all elements in a slide, click the Slide Sorter view button and then click the slide. To specify individual slide elements for animation, switch to Normal view or Slide view and then click the element.

2. Choose View⇨Toolbars⇨Animation Effects from the Menu bar to make the Animation Effects toolbar appear.

3. Click the desired animation options on the Animation Effects
toolbar.

Adding Movies and Motion Clips

PowerPoint offers you the option of adding small movies to slides
in your presentation. You can also choose to add a special kind of
animated movie called a *motion clip* from PowerPoint's accompa-
nying Clip Gallery.

A movie clip takes up tons of memory and can really drag down
the performance of your computer. File sizes are typically 1MB or
more, even for a teensy-weensy movie snippet. I generally don't
use movies except on an occasional wake-up slide or for a moment
of humor.

Choosing the correct movie file format

Movies come in a variety of file formats, so check to be sure that
your system is capable of playing the popular types that you may
want to incorporate into your PowerPoint presentations. Common
movie formats include:

- ✦ **MOV and QT:** This is a QuickTime movie, which is probably
  the most prevalent audio/movie file format.

- ✦ **AVI:** This file type is used by Movie for Windows. AVI inter-
  leaves audio and video, which yields a smaller file size than
  QuickTime. Because this format is most often used in Windows-
  based programs, it is the most reliable format.

- ✦ **MPEG, MPG, and MPE:** MPEG is both a movie file format and
  a compression/decompression standard. MPEG movies
  compress to much smaller file sizes than QT and AVI, but
  MPEG movies may require special decoding software and
  hardware for playback.

Adding a motion clip from the Clip Gallery

The following steps tell you how to add a motion clip from the Clip
Gallery to your slide:

1. In Slide view or Normal view, move to the slide where you
want to add a motion clip.

2. Choose Insert➪Movies and Sounds➪Movie from Gallery. An
Insert Movie dialog box appears with the Motion Clips tab
selected.

3. Click a category of clips and then click a motion clip to select it.

4. Click Insert Clip. The motion clip is inserted right in the middle of your slide.

5. (Optional) Resize the motion clip and reposition it by dragging it to a new location. Because a motion clip is both heard *and* seen, you need to give it some room to physically reside on your slide. Be aware that you may need to rearrange slide elements — text boxes, clip art, and other objects — to accommodate an added motion clip.

When not playing, the motion clip shows only the first frame as a placeholder on the slide where it is located. In this sense, the motion clip appears similar to other graphic elements on a slide. Start the slide show and move to the motion clip–embellished slide to see how the motion clip appears while playing.

Adding a movie from a file

The following steps show you how to add a movie from a file to your slide:

1. In Slide view or Normal view, move to the slide where you want to add a movie.

2. Choose Insert⇨Movies and Sounds⇨Movie from File from the Menu bar. The Insert Movie dialog box appears.

3. Find and click the movie you want to add and click OK. The movie is inserted right in the middle of your slide.

4. PowerPoint asks whether you want the movie to play automatically in the slide show. Click Yes to make the movie play automatically on the slide or click No to play the movie only when you click it.

5. (Optional) Resize the movie and reposition it by dragging it to a new location.

When not playing, the movie shows only the first frame as a placeholder on the slide where it is located.

Many commercial CD-ROMs offer short movie clips designed for use in PowerPoint presentations. You can also find several movies available for download from the Internet.

Playing a movie

You can play many movies in Normal view or Slide view simply by double-clicking them. Motion clips added from the Clip Gallery, however, won't play in Normal view or Slide view.

If you're running the slide show presentation, just single-click the movie to play it. If you chose to have the movie play automatically, it begins playing when you reach the slide where it resides.

While a movie plays, you can click the movie to pause it.

Adding Pictures: Clip Art and Photos

Pictures take the form of either clip art or photos:

+ **Clip art:** Line drawings composed of lines, ovals, squares, and all sorts of other shapes. The component shapes of a clip art image are electronically glued together (in other words, *grouped*) to form the final piece of clip art. A piece of clip art can be broken down into its individual shapes, and each of these shapes can be edited separately. *See also* "Grouping, Ungrouping, and Regrouping Clips" later in this part.

+ **Photos:** Images are composed of rows and columns of colored dots (called *pixels*). Photos can't be separated into their component elements, except with a photo-editing program, like PhotoShop.

You can find pictures in the Clip Gallery that comes with PowerPoint, the Clip Gallery Live that PowerPoint users can access on the Internet, and clip art collections that you can buy in stores or find on the Internet.

Choosing the correct file format

PowerPoint allows you to include a wide selection of graphics file formats in your presentations. The following formats can be incorporated directly, without the aid of separate graphics filters:

✦ **BMP, RLE, and DIB:** Bitmap, a popular Windows format; tends to have large file sizes

✦ **EMF:** Enhanced Metafile

✦ **GIF:** Graphics Interchange Format; common on the Internet; lower-quality images than JPG

✦ **JPG:** JPEG (Joint Photographic Experts Group) format; common on the Internet

✦ **PNG:** Portable Network Graphics

✦ **WMF:** Windows Metafile

The following graphics file formats can also be used, but they require separate filters:

✦ **CDR:** CorelDRAW

✦ **CGM:** Computer Graphics Metafile

✦ **EPS:** Encapsulated PostScript

✦ **FPX:** FlashPix

✦ **JSH, JAH, and JBH:** Hanako

✦ **PCD:** Kodak Photo CD

✦ **PCT:** Macintosh PICT

✦ **PCX:** PC Paintbrush

✦ **TIF:** Tagged Image File Format

✦ **WPG:** WordPerfect Graphics

If the necessary filters aren't installed, rerun the PowerPoint Setup to add the filters. For information about how to install program components, see *Windows 95 For Dummies* or *Windows 98 For Dummies,* both by Andy Rathbone, and both published by IDG Books Worldwide, Inc.

Adding a picture from the Clip Gallery

The following steps tell you how to add a piece of clip art or a photo from the Clip Gallery to your slide:

1. In Slide view or Normal view, move to the slide where you want to add a picture.

2. Choose Insert⇨Picture⇨Clip Art from the Menu bar or click the Insert Clip Art button on the Drawing toolbar. An Insert Clip Art dialog box appears with the Pictures tab selected.

3. Click a category of clips, then click a piece of clip art or a photo to select it.

4. Click Insert Clip. The picture is inserted right in the middle of your slide.

5. (Optional) Resize the picture and reposition it by dragging it to a new location.

Adding a picture from a file

The following steps show you how to add a picture from a file to your slide:

1. In Slide view or Normal view, move to the slide where you want to add a picture.

2. Choose Insert⇨Picture⇨From File from the Menu bar. The Insert Picture dialog box appears.

3. Find and click the picture you want to add and click OK. The picture is inserted right in the middle of your slide.

4. (Optional) Resize the movie and reposition it by dragging it to a new location.

Adding Polygons and Freeform Shapes

For those occasions when a regular ol' square or circle just doesn't cut it, you may want to create a more elaborate polygon or even a wild freeform shape. Create such beasts using the following steps:

1. On the Drawing toolbar, choose AutoShapes⇨Lines. A palette of line types appears. Click the Freeform button.

2. Click your slide at the spot where you want to start drawing your object.

3. Release the mouse button and drag the mouse to form a straight line segment, or hold the mouse button down and drag to draw freehand.

Holding down the Shift key as you draw causes straight lines to form in increments of 15-degree angles: horizontal, at a 15-degree incline, at a 30-degree incline, at a 45-degree incline, at a 60-degree incline, at a 75-degree incline, or vertical.

4. If you want to draw a straight line segment, click the mouse button to create a corner and redirect your line. If you're drawing freehand, release the mouse button to create a corner and redirect your line.

5. Complete your shape by double-clicking.

Double-clicking in close proximity to your starting point forms a closed figure. Otherwise, you form an open figure.

Your shape automatically fills with color. ***See also*** "Choosing line colors or patterns" and "Filling Shapes with Color and Patterns," later in this part, to adjust the line and fill colors and line thickness.

Double-click your finished shape to edit each of its component curves and turns.

Adding Rectangles, Squares, Ovals, and Circles

PowerPoint lets you create all sorts of rectangles, squares, ovals, and circles like those shown in the following figure.

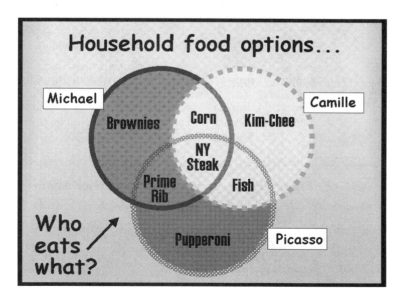

To draw a rectangular (or square) or oval (or circular) shape, follow these steps:

1. Click the appropriate button:

• **Rectangle or square:** Click the Rectangle button. To draw a square, hold down the Shift key in Steps 2 and 3.

• **Oval or circle:** Click the Oval button. To draw a circle, hold down the Shift key in Steps 2 and 3.

2. Click and hold the spot where you want to position the top-left boundary of the shape.

3. Drag to create the shape in the size you choose.

4. Release the mouse when your shape attains the desired proportions.

You can adjust the size and dimensions of your shape by clicking the created shape and then grabbing and dragging one of its resizing handles.

Adding Sound

Adding music, sound effects, and other audio snippets to your PowerPoint slides electrifies your presentation more than mere text and images alone can. PowerPoint comes with a small library of sound files that you can raid whenever you need a foghorn, phone ring, or rooster. You can find more sounds on the Internet (even beyond Clip Gallery Live), where you can locate Web sites offering sound clips for virtually every sound imaginable.

Sound files take up a fair amount of disk space. Each second of sound can occupy 10K or more — a small enough space to make use of sound, but not so small a space that you can go completely nuts with it. Use sound as an embellishment, but don't incorporate 5-minute-long show tunes in your slides, or you'll blow out your processor — and your memory.

Choosing the correct file format

PowerPoint can play several formats of sound files. No one particular sound file format is preferable to any other:

✦ **WAV:** Digitized recordings of real sounds, like a baby crying, a bird tweeting, or a toilet flushing

✦ **MID:** MIDI music stored in a form that the sound card's synthesizer can play

✦ **AU:** Common audio files found on the Internet

✦ **AIFF:** Also common on the Internet

Adding a sound from the Clip Gallery

Inserting a sound into a PowerPoint presentation is as simple as making your choice and pasting that choice onto a slide. When you run the slide show, you can set up the sounds to play either during slide transitions or at the click of a Sound icon. **See also** Part VII for more information on running the slide show.

1. Move to the slide that you want to jazz up with sound.

2. Choose Insert⟹Movies and Sounds⟹Sound from Gallery. The Clip Gallery dialog box appears with the Sounds tab selected.

3. Scroll through the list of Clip Gallery sounds until you find the one you're looking for; then click the sound to select it.

4. Click Insert. The sound is pasted on the slide. Notice that a little sound icon appears on the slide to show you that your sound has been added.

Click to hear the rooster crow

Adding a sound from another source

If you want to insert a sound that hasn't been cataloged in the Clip Gallery (such as one you downloaded from the Internet, or one you digitized and stored yourself), just follow these steps:

1. Move to the slide where you want to add a sound.

2. Choose Insert⟹Movies and Sounds⟹Sound from File. The Insert Sound dialog box appears.

3. Find and click the sound you want to add and click OK. The sound is inserted as a little sound icon right in the middle of your slide. A dialog box appears, asking whether you want the sound to play automatically.

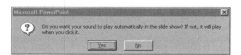

4. Click Yes if you want the sound to play automatically or No if you want the sound to play only when you click its icon during the slide show.

Playing an added sound

To play a sound you added as you're working in Slide view, double-click the sound icon.

To play the sound during a slide show presentation, click the sound icon whenever it appears on a slide (unless you choose to have the sound play automatically on a slide).

You can also cause sounds to play in between slides (during a slide transition). *See also* Part VII.

Adding WordArt

WordArt is a nifty feature that allows you to place fancy, three-dimensional, shadowed text on your slides. The text can even be given a perspective quality, as if you're standing at the H looking toward the rest of the letters in the HOLLYWOOD sign.

WordArt text is created using the WordArt button on the Drawing toolbar, which summons a collection of WordArt style thumbnails and a special typing window. After selecting a style and typing in your desired text, your WordArt creation is transferred to your PowerPoint slide as a drawing object. Each WordArt object can be manipulated much like any other drawing object — it can be stretched, skewed, rotated, and filled with any color or texture you choose.

Because WordArt clips don't function like editable text, they don't appear in Outline view and they can't be spell-checked.

To add a WordArt clip to a slide, follow these steps:

1. On the Drawing toolbar, click the WordArt button. The WordArt Gallery dialog box appears.

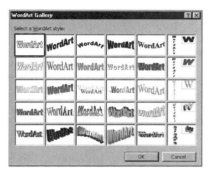

2. Click the thumbnail representing the WordArt style that you want to use and click OK. An Edit WordArt Text dialog box appears.

3. In the Edit WordArt Text dialog box, type your text, select a font and point size, and choose bold or italic formatting options. Click OK. The WordArt text is placed on your slide.

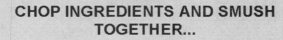

- 1 huge avocado
- 2 slices lemon
- 1 scallion

- 1/2 tomato
- 1/8 clove garlic
- salt to taste

CHOP INGREDIENTS AND SMUSH TOGETHER...

SERVE WITH CHIPS!

To edit your WordArt, use the tools on the Drawing toolbar. For additional WordArt editing tools, select View⇨Toolbars⇨WordArt from the Menu bar, and the WordArt toolbar appears. The WordArt toolbar offers several tools for editing your WordArt clip.

WordArt Toolbar Button	What It Does
Edit Text...	Opens a dialog box for editing WordArt text
◀	Opens a dialog box for editing WordArt styles
✎	Opens a dialog box for editing WordArt line and fill colors
Abc	Opens a palette for selecting WordArt shapes
↻	Provides handles for rotating WordArt clips

WordArt Toolbar Button	What It Does
Aa	Toggles WordArt letters between varying and uniform heights
Ab bⱼ	Toggles WordArt clips between horizontal and vertical orientation
≣	Provides choices for aligning WordArt clips
AV	Provides kerning choices of WordArt letters

Creating 3-D Effects

The 3-D button, which lets you turn flat shapes into 3-D shapes without putting those gaudy red and blue glasses over your eyes, is great for showing perspective and for creating a sense of relative position.

Add 3-D effects to a shape as follows:

1. Select the shape by clicking it.

 2. Click the 3-D button on the Drawing toolbar and click a 3-D effect from the palette of 3-D effects that appears.

Click 3-D Settings to summon a toolbar that allows you to adjust the tilt, depth, lighting, and texture of the 3-D effects.

Deleting a Clip

To remove a clip

1. Select the clip by clicking it.

2. Press the Delete key to blow it away.

If you suddenly realize that your deletion was a horrible mistake, choose Edit⇨Undo, or press Ctrl+Z, to get your clip back.

Drawing Lines

PowerPoint allows you to make your mark using a variety of different line styles.

Straight lines

These steps show you how to draw a straight line:

1. Click the Line button on the Drawing toolbar, or choose AutoShapes⇨Lines, and then click the Line button.

2. Click and hold the mouse where you want the line to start.

3. Drag the mouse to create a line of the desired length and position, and release the mouse when you reach the end of the line.

Holding down the Shift key as you draw the line forces the line to be drawn in 15-degree increments: horizontal; in 15, 30, 45, 60, or 75 degrees of inclination; or vertical.

Curved lines

To draw a curved line

1. On the Drawing toolbar, choose AutoShapes⇨Lines and then click the Curve button.

2. Click your slide where you want the curve to start; then start drawing. You don't need to hold down the mouse button as you draw.

3. Click each time you want to create a turn or bend in your line (you can add as many turns as you want).

4. Double-click to end the line. Double-clicking in close proximity to your starting point creates a closed figure.

Freehand lines

To draw a freehand (squiggly) line

1. On the Drawing toolbar, choose AutoShapes⇨Lines and then click the Scribble button.

2. Click and drag the mouse to create your line.

3. Release the mouse button to end the line.

Changing line style

After you draw a line, you can change its style — making it thin or thick, solid or dashed, and with or without arrows.

To set the line style, click the line that you want to change. Then click one of the following buttons on the Drawing toolbar:

✦ **Line Style button:** When you click the Line Style button on the drawing toolbar, a line style menu appears. You can choose a new thickness, or select the <u>M</u>ore Lines command, which provides you with millions of other choices in a dialog box.

✦ **Dash Style button:** Choose a new dash style if you want to use something other than a solid line. The Dash Style button on the Drawing toolbar opens a menu that lets you select whether your line appears as a series of dots, short dashes, long dashes, or dots alternating with dashes. Sort of like Morse code!

✦ **Arrow Style button:** Choose arrows as end points for your line. Click the Arrow Style button on the Drawing toolbar to call up a menu including a <u>M</u>ore Arrows command that provides additional arrow options.

Choosing line colors or patterns

Use the following steps to alter the color or pattern of a line:

1. Click the line that you want to color. You can also click a shape in order to color the line that creates the shape's boundary.

2. Click the down arrow to the right of the Line Color button on the Drawing toolbar; then click a color or a pattern from the pop-up menu.

Choosing a pattern means that your line has a combination of two colors. These two colors may appear together as small dots on a solid background, interweaving lines, or other options. It may be difficult to clearly see this pattern if your line is very thin — thicker lines show patterns more effectively.

Drawing with AutoShapes

Selecting the PowerPoint AutoShapes menu from the Drawing toolbar produces a pop-up list from which you can choose predrawn line styles and common shapes, like hexagons, banners, moons, and flowchart arrows.

To add a shape to your slide using AutoShapes, just follow these steps:

1. Select the AutoShapes menu on the Drawing toolbar. A veritable shopping mall of shape selections appears.

You can make the AutoShapes menu into a floating palette by clicking the top of the box and dragging it away from the Drawing toolbar.

2. Select the AutoShapes category that you want:

* **Lines:** Every type of line from straight to swervy. You can also build closed-line figures.

* **Connectors:** Line segments with strangely shaped end points. Commonly used for road maps and electrical circuits.

* **Basic Shapes:** Hearts, moons, and parallelograms. Get yer Lucky Charms here, laddy!

* **Block Arrows:** Directions such as north, south, and U-turn.

* **Flowchart:** Directional signs which track the flow of money from the wallets of your consumers, into the profit pool of your company, and out to the wallets of your shareholders.

* **Stars and Banners:** For patriots and American history teachers.

* **Callouts:** You can type text inside these shapes; the text may describe an image the shape is pointing to or represents what the image is saying or thinking.

* **Action Buttons:** Navigation icons for slide-show and Web-based presentations. Some of these little guys resemble buttons on your VCR. *See also* Part VII for more information.

* **More AutoShapes:** Summons the Microsoft Clip Gallery where you can obtain additional AutoShapes.

3. Click a shape featured in the category.

4. Create your chosen shape by clicking your slide and dragging the mouse until your AutoShapes clip reaches the desired size.

To maintain the same height-to-width proportions when you resize an AutoShapes clip, hold down the Shift key as you drag the mouse.

Several AutoShapes have special handles that allow you to change the proportions of the AutoShapes clip. For example, when you create shapes like parallelograms, you can adjust the handle to tip the parallelogram over a little or a lot.

5. Release the mouse button to finish creating your AutoShapes clip.

To change the AutoShape option you want to use (but to keep the color and all the other attributes you selected for the object), click AutoShape and then choose Draw⇨Change AutoShape. Select a new AutoShape from the pop-up palette. The AutoShape changes according to your choice.

Editing Clip Art

You may sometimes find a clip art image that almost meets your needs, but isn't perfect. All you need to do to whip the clip art into the precise image you need is a bit of tweaking.

To edit the clip art, follow these steps:

1. Select the clip art that you want to edit by clicking it.

2. Choose Draw⇨Ungroup from the Drawing toolbar and answer Yes when PowerPoint asks you if you want to convert your clip art to a PowerPoint object. *See also* "Grouping, Ungrouping, and Regrouping Clips" later in this part for more information.

3. Edit the clip art by clicking each element that you want to change; then use the drawing tools to adjust the attributes of the element.

4. To group the picture, select all of the elements in the original group and then choose Draw⇨Group from the Drawing toolbar. You can now click and drag your newly edited clip art wherever you like.

Enhancing Images

Love the picture but hate the colors? Then do unto your picture as Ted Turner hath done to many a movie classic: Colorize it.

The Picture toolbar offers a variety of tools for performing basic image-enhancing tasks such as recoloring, adjusting contrast and brightness, cropping, and making a color transparent. Choose View⇨Toolbars from the Menu bar and click the Picture option to make the Picture toolbar appear.

The Picture toolbar is no PhotoShop, but it can perform a few simple functions that can improve the look of your pictures. *See also* the PowerPoint Help menu for additional details on working with each of these features.

Changing clip art colors

PowerPoint allows you to selectively change any or all colors in your chosen clip art. Recolor clip art as follows:

1. Click the clip art that you want to recolor.

2. Click the Recolor Picture button on the Picture toolbar to open the Recolor Picture dialog box.

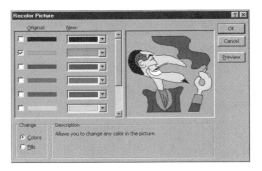

3. In the Original column, click the check box beside the color that you want to change.

4. Click the New drop-down list box beside your selected original color and click a new color to replace the original color.

5. Repeat Steps 3 and 4 until you modify every color that you want to change.

6. Click OK to complete the recolor process.

Changing contrast and brightness of photos

PowerPoint doesn't have a tool for changing individual colors on a photo, but it does provide four buttons on the Picture toolbar for tweaking the contrast and brightness of an entire photo. Just click the photo that you want to work on; then click one of the following buttons on the Picture toolbar:

♦ **More Contrast button:** Increases the contrast of the photo

♦ **Less Contrast button:** Decreases the contrast of the photo; good for reducing the distraction caused by a photo you may use for a background for text

♦ **More Brightness button:** Increases the brightness of the photo; good for lightening a photo you may want to use as a background for dark-colored text

♦ **Less Brightness button:** Decreases the brightness of the photo; good for darkening a photo you may use as a background for light-colored text

If you're unhappy with your picture-tweaking efforts, click the Reset Picture button on the Picture toolbar to make your picture revert back to its original contrast and brightness.

Filling Shapes with Color and Patterns

Coloring within the lines has never been easier. PowerPoint offers you several coloring options, including filling a shape with solid or semitransparent color, shaded blends of two colors, and patterns of two colors.

1. Select the shape that you want to color by clicking it.

2. Click the down arrow to the right of the Fill Color button on the Drawing toolbar and click a color from the selection that appears. Note that you can also select No Fill, More Fill Colors, and Fill Effects that allow you to access fill gradients, patterns, and textures.

Choosing the More Fill Colors option summons a Colors dialog box in which you can choose a color and also check the Semitransparent fill check box. Checking the semitransparent option gives your object a see-through quality in which lower layers of objects can be seen partially peeking through.

Flipping Clips

Flipping a PowerPoint clip creates a mirror image of the clip. You can flip clips horizontally or vertically:

♦ Flipping clips horizontally makes an eastward-flying airplane and gaggle of geese appear as if they reversed course and started flying westward.

✦ Flipping clips vertically makes a moon-bound rocket look as if it's now headed back toward Earth.

To flip a PowerPoint clip, just follow these steps:

1. Select the clip that you want to flip by clicking it.

2. Tell PowerPoint which way you want to flip the clip by choosing either Draw➪Rotate or Flip➪Flip Horizontal or Draw➪Rotate or Flip➪Flip Vertical.

Grouping, Ungrouping, and Regrouping Clips

Grouping allows you to create and work on simple shapes and then combine them into a more complex image. By combining, or grouping, several smaller clips into a single larger one, you can treat the grouped clip as a single entity, which is particularly helpful when you're moving or resizing the grouped clips — without grouping, you have to move or resize each little component element one by one.

To create a group, follow these steps:

1. Select the clips that you want to group by using one of these methods:

   • **Shift-click each clip:** Hold down the Shift key and click each individual item that you want as part of the group.

- **Box in all the clips:** Click near — but not on — the items that you want to group. Then drag the mouse to create a picture frame around your items. After you complete your frame, release the mouse button.

2. Choose Draw⇨Group from the Drawing toolbar to group your clips. The sizing handles on each individual item vanish and are replaced by sizing handles for the new group.

You may wish to ungroup a grouped clip for the purpose of editing specific elements of the group. To ungroup a grouped clip, follow these steps:

1. Select the grouped clip by clicking it.

2. Choose Draw⇨Ungroup from Drawing toolbar to ungroup the selected object.

After a grouped clip is ungrouped, it identifies each of its component objects by placing resizing handles around each clip. You may have to ungroup several times to reach a point where none of the clips are grouped.

To regroup a previous grouping:

1. Click any of the clips that were part of the original group.

2. Choose Draw⇨Regroup from the Drawing toolbar. PowerPoint regroups the objects, recalling your previous grouping.

 Group clips that belong in the same layer, particularly if you're moving layers forward and backward to obtain certain physical relationships. *See* "Layering Clips" in this part for the details.

Layering Clips

Layering is a powerful tool for creating perspective and conveying visual relationships. It shuffles the order in which clips appear on-screen, allowing you to choose which clips appear in front and behind each other. For example, you can move a palm tree from in front of a house to behind the house to show the house more clearly.

Available layering commands include:

✦ **Bring to Front:** Brings the selected clip (and all other clips with which it is grouped) to the topmost layer of the slide. All other layers appear behind or underneath the selected clip.

✦ **Send to Back:** Sends the selected clip (and all other clips with which it is grouped) to the bottom layer of the slide. All other layers appear in front of or on top of the selected clip.

✦ **Bring Forward:** Brings the selected clip (and all other clips with which it is grouped) one layer up (or higher) on the slide.

✦ **Send Backward:** Sends the selected clip (and all other clips with which it is grouped) one layer down (or lower) on the slide.

To change the layer in which a clip hangs out:

1. Click the clip to select it.

2. On the Drawing toolbar, choose Draw➪Order and one of the layering commands.

When you're working with complex drawing clips, first group clips that belong together. Then click each group and move it forward or backward to its proper layer.

Lining Up Clips with Guides

PowerPoint provides a set of horizontal and vertical crosshairs that aid you in lining up clips on your slides. These guides serve the same helpful purpose as grid lines on a sheet of graph paper. When you drag a clip close to a guide, the clip automatically aligns its edge to fit snugly against the guide. When you drag a clip close to the intersection of two guides, the clip automatically aligns its center at the guides' point of intersection.

If you're working in Normal view or Slide view, activate the guides by choosing View➪Guides from the Menu bar. The guides are initially positioned so that they cross at the geometric center of the slide — a position labeled as (0,0). To measure precisely where the guides are positioned, turn on the ruler (*see* "Lining Up Clips with the Ruler" later in this part for details).

Each guide may be moved by clicking it and dragging it to a new position. As you move a guide up and down, a numerical marker that indicates its vertical position in inches appears. As you move a guide left and right, a numerical marker that indicates its horizontal position in inches appears.

You can add a new guide by clicking an existing guide, pressing Ctrl, and dragging the new guide away. You can delete a guide by dragging it toward the edge of the slide: After it reaches the edge, it vanishes.

✦ To automatically align clips with guides, choose Draw⟳ Snap⟳To Grid on the Drawing toolbar.

✦ To automatically align objects with guides that run through the horizontal and vertical edges of other shapes, choose Draw⟳Snap⟳To Shape on the Drawing toolbar.

Lining Up Clips with the Ruler

You may never require the precision that PowerPoint's ruler can provide (I never do), but if you're a perfectionist, you can use the ruler to align shapes and images on your slide.

If you're working in Normal view or Slide view, activate the ruler by choosing View⟳Ruler from the Menu bar. Two rulers magically appear:

✦ **Horizontal:** The ruler along the top of your slide window. The zero position marks the horizontal half-way location on your slide.

✦ **Vertical:** The ruler along the left side of your slide window. The zero position marks the vertical half-way location on your slide.

When the rulers are displayed, your pointer position or cursor position is tracked on both the horizontal and vertical rulers. That way, as you drag clips around the screen, you know the exact numerical position of the upper-left corner of each clip.

You can use this cursor tracking to accurately position your on-screen clips. For example, you can locate the upper-left corner of each of four movie clips at three inches above the zero mark on the vertical ruler.

Lining Up Clips with Alignment Commands

PowerPoint provides many alignment commands that allow you to set the alignment of clips on your slides. Clips can be aligned with other clips, or they can be aligned relative to a slide edge.

You can also arrange or distribute clips so that they are spaced equally apart from one another — horizontally, vertically, or relative to the entire slide.

Aligning clips with other clips

Aligning a set of clips relative to others is very easy. For example, you can line up a series of clips vertically, with equal spacing along a central axis (sort of like the way the rings of a toddler's ring toy stack up on a standing pole). Another way you can align clips is by their edges, like pushing boxes of different sizes so they all rest flush against a wall. In Normal view or Slide view, select the clip that you want to align by pressing and holding Shift and clicking each clip. Then select any of the following options on the Drawing toolbar:

- ✦ **By the left edge:** Draw⇨Align or Distribute⇨Align Left

- ✦ **By the right edge:** Draw⇨Align or Distribute⇨Align Right

- ✦ **Horizontally by the center:** Draw⇨Align or Distribute⇨ Align Center

- ✦ **Vertically by the middle:** Draw⇨Align or Distribute⇨ Align Middle

- ✦ **By the top edge:** Draw⇨Align or Distribute⇨Align Top

- ✦ **By the bottom edge:** Draw⇨Align or Distribute⇨Align Bottom

Aligning clips with the entire slide

Aligning clips with the entire slide is similar to aligning clips with each other. The difference is this: aligning clips by their middles also aligns them with the central axis of the slide; aligning clips by their bottoms also aligns them with the bottom of the slide; and so on. To align clips with the entire slide, follow these steps:

1. In Normal view or Slide view, select the clips that you want to align by pressing and holding Shift and clicking each clip.

2. On the Drawing toolbar, choose D̲raw⇨A̲lign or Distribute⇨ Relative to S̲lide to place a check mark next to this option.

3. On the Drawing toolbar, choose D̲raw⇨A̲lign or Distribute and then click the option that you want to employ in aligning the clips. *See* "Aligning clips with other clips" earlier in this part for available options.

Distributing clips equal distances from one another or relative to the entire slide

To place clips at equal distances from each other or to distribute them uniformly all over the slide (like planting ears of corn in 1-foot increments from each other throughout an entire field), follow these steps:

1. In Normal view or Slide view, select the clips that you want to distribute by pressing and holding Shift and clicking each clip.

2. To arrange clips equal distances from each other, choose D̲raw⇨A̲lign or Distribute on the Drawing toolbar, and select either the Distribute H̲orizontally option or the Distribute V̲ertically option.

3. To arrange clips equal distances from each other relative to the entire slide, make sure that the Relative to S̲lide option is checked. Then select D̲raw⇨A̲lign or Distribute on the Drawing toolbar, and select either the Distribute H̲orizontally option or the Distribute V̲ertically option.

Nudging a clip

Sometimes, after aligning clips, you discover that you don't want things quite so cut-and-dried. If you need to move a clip just a smidgen, use these nudging steps:

1. In Normal view or Slide view, select the clip that you want to nudge by clicking it.

2. On the Drawing toolbar, choose D̲raw⇨N̲udge and the direction you wish to nudge the clip: up, down, left, or right.

You can also press an arrow key to nudge a selected clip in the desired direction.

Moving and Resizing Clips

PowerPoint adds clips to your slides the same way that the cafeteria worker adds food to your tray in the buffet line: glopped down smack dab in the middle. You may want to move your clip to a more appetizing location, as well as stretch or shrink it to fit nicely on your slide.

When you insert a clip, it appears on your screen as a selected clip — with resizing handles surrounding it like a picture frame. If you click outside the clip, the handles vanish. Click the clip once to make the handles reappear. Handles must be visible to move and resize your clip.

You can move or resize your clips as follows:

✦ **Move the clip:** Click it once and drag it to a new spot.

✦ **Enlarge the clip:** Click a corner handle and drag the handle outwards from the clip.

✦ **Shrink the clip:** Click a corner handle and drag the handle in toward the clip.

✦ **Make the clip taller or shorter without changing the width:** Click a top or bottom center handle and drag the handle up or down.

✦ **Make the clip wider or narrower without changing the height:** Click a left or right center handle and drag the handle horizontally.

Rotating Clips

Rotating is turning a clip around a central axis. Rotating is particularly useful for making standing clips appear as if they fell over: A 90-degree rotation in either direction gets the job done. Rotating is also good for creating a sense of action. A picture of a car on a flat road suddenly conveys motion when you rotate it, with the car appearing either to climb a steep incline or to speed down a sloping hill.

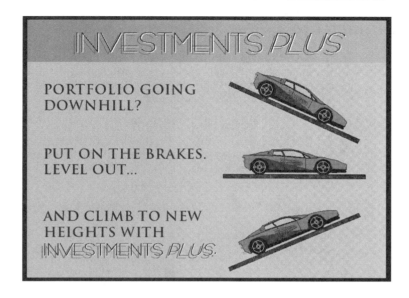

Rotate a clip by following these steps:

1. Select the clip to be rotated by clicking it.

2. Tell PowerPoint which way you want the clip rotated:

- **To rotate your clip left 90 degrees:** Choose Draw⇨Rotate or Flip⇨Rotate Left from the Drawing toolbar. Rotating left turns the clip 90 degrees counterclockwise.

- **To rotate your clip right 90 degrees:** Choose Draw⇨Rotate or Flip⇨Rotate Right from the Drawing toolbar. Rotating right turns the clip 90 degrees clockwise.

- **To rotate your shape freely:** Choose Draw⇨Rotate or Flip⇨Free Rotate; then just grab one of the corner rotation handles on your shape and turn your clip clockwise or counterclockwise. Free rotation allows you to rotate your clip at any degree angle.

Note: Rotating a clip 180 degrees is *not* the same as flipping a clip. Rotating 180 degrees turns the clip upside-down, whereas flipping creates a mirror image. *See also* "Flipping Clips" earlier in this part.

Shadowing Clips

Shadowing a clip allows you to add depth to the shape by making it appear as if it is casting a shadow. You can adjust how much shadow is generated and where the shadow falls. To add a shadow to a shape, just follow these steps:

1. Click the shape that you want to shadow.

 2. Click the Shadow button on the Drawing toolbar and a palette of shadow options appears. Click the box that represents your desired shadow effect.

Note that this palette offers the option of turning off the shadow by clicking No Shadow, and fine-tuning shadow details by clicking Shadow Settings.

Part VI

Showing Your Business Savvy

In the world of art, a picture is worth a thousand words. In the world of business, a picture of your data — in charts, graphs, equations, spreadsheets, or tables — is worth a thousand bucks.

This part addresses how to create the best darn graphs and organizational charts for display in PowerPoint, along with how to insert complex equations and spreadsheets into your presentation with minimal effort. Additionally, you also find out how to use PowerPoint's special tools for recording minutes and notes during a meeting, and for generating an action item "to-do" list at the conclusion of a meeting. I also tell you how to create speaker notes to aid you in giving your presentation.

In this part . . .

- ✔ **Building a graph**
- ✔ **Creating an organizational chart**
- ✔ **Generating tables**
- ✔ **Importing spreadsheets**
- ✔ **Making equations with Equation Editor**
- ✔ **Recording meeting minutes and action items**
- ✔ **Improving your performance using speaker notes**

Creating Graphs

PowerPoint includes a program called Microsoft Graph that you can use to convert numerical information into pie graphs, bar graphs, and even some exotic things called cone graphs, not to be confused with the Coneheads. You don't have to do anything special to access Microsoft Graph — the program starts up immediately whenever you choose to create a graph in PowerPoint.

Note: Microsoft programs refer to *graphs* and *charts* interchangeably — a habit I consider incredibly confusing. This book always refers to an object built by Microsoft Graph as a *graph* and always refers to an organizational chart as a *chart.* And never the twain shall meet.

 While working in Microsoft Graph, you may notice that many new graph-related buttons appear on your Standard toolbar. You may also observe that certain menu functions change on the Menu bar. These buttons and menu item changes vanish after you exit the Graph program.

Adding a slide with a graph placeholder

To create a new slide on which you intend to place a graph, follow these steps:

1. In Slide view, Normal view, or Slide Sorter view, move to the location in your presentation where you want to insert a new slide with a graph.

 2. Choose Insert⇨New Slide from the Menu bar, click the New Slide button on the Standard Toolbar, or press Ctrl+M. The New Slide dialog box appears.

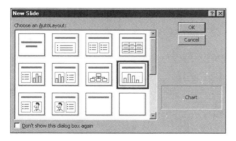

3. Select an AutoLayout design that includes a graph and click OK. Unfortunately, the description of the AutoLayout in the dialog box refers to the graph as a *chart.* Just ignore it. A new slide appears with a placeholder for a graph.

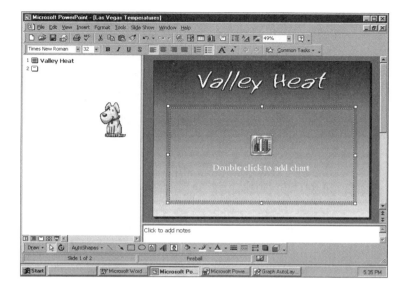

4. Double-click the graph placeholder to begin building your graph. Microsoft Graph opens and displays a sample graph accompanied by a sample datasheet.

5. Input your own data into the datasheet, which works like a spreadsheet. *See also* "Using the datasheet" later in this part for more details.

6. Close your datasheet by clicking the X in the upper-right corner of the sheet.

7. Click outside the graph area to return to the slide. The graph is redrawn with the data you entered in the datasheet.

See also "Labeling a graph" later in this part.

Adding a graph to an existing slide

To add a graph to a slide already in your presentation

1. In Slide view or Normal view, move to the slide where you want to add a graph.

 2. Click the Insert Chart button on the Standard toolbar or choose Insert➪Chart from the Menu bar. A sample datasheet and graph appear on the slide.

3. Replace the data in the sample datasheet with your actual information. *See also* "Using the datasheet" later in this part for details.

4. Close your datasheet by clicking the X in the upper-right corner of the datasheet.

5. Click outside the graph area to return to the slide. The graph is redrawn with the data you entered in the datasheet.

See also "Moving and resizing a graph," "Labeling a graph," and "Graphing options" later in this part.

Using the datasheet

Microsoft Graph uses information you supply in a datasheet to construct the graph that ultimately ends up (looking beautiful) on your slide. The datasheet functions as a simple spreadsheet, providing rows and columns where you insert your data. Rows are designated by numbers, and columns are designated by letters. Each data point you enter is cubbyholed in a unique cell of the datasheet.

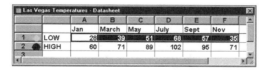

The following list gives you a few tips about working with the datasheet:

✦ Simply click a cell and type to enter information into the cell.

 ✦ You can banish the datasheet by simply closing its window. You can make your datasheet reappear at any time by clicking the View Datasheet button on the Standard toolbar.

✦ The datasheet reserves the first row and column for headings that are used to label the resulting graph, so don't attempt to enter any numerical data in these cells.

✦ The datasheet doesn't allow you to perform certain spread-sheet operations, such as using formulas. See "Importing Worksheets and Charts from Excel," later in this part, for information on working with more advanced spreadsheet operations.

✦ Depending on how much room your data cells require, you may want to adjust the column width of the datasheet by choosing Format⇨Column Width from the Menu bar. Column width is for your ease when working in the datasheet — adjusting column widths doesn't change the graph itself.

✦ You may also want to reformat the types of numbers in the datasheet by choosing Format➪Number from the Menu bar and selecting from options such as Percent, Scientific, and Currency. As with any spreadsheet-style program, using the Format command assists you in entering and manipulating a variety of number types.

Graphing options

After filling your datasheet with numbers, you can transform those numbers into a graph suitable for display. Microsoft Graph offers you 14 graph types, from the frequently used (line and scatter) to the weird (bubble, cone, and tube) and the really strange (doughnut and radar). It also offers you a handful of unusual, custom graph types in case none of the standard types suit your needs. Try out several graph types for your data before you choose the one that best conveys the information to your audience.

To choose a graph type after completing your datasheet

1. Double-click the graph on the slide to activate the Microsoft Graph program. If you're already working in Microsoft Graph, just single-click the graph you see on-screen to select it.

2. Choose Chart➪Chart Type from the Menu bar to open the Chart Type dialog box.

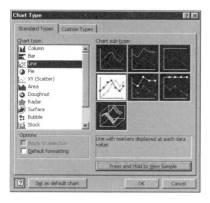

3. Click either the Standard Types tab or the Custom Types tab.

4. Choose a graph style by selecting an option in the Chart type area. On the Standard Types tab, you may also click an option in the Chart sub-type area, which offers variations on the Standard theme.

For the Standard Types tab, you can obtain a thumbnail preview of how your data appears in a selected graph type by clicking the View Sample button. For the Custom Types tab, a thumbnail preview of your data automatically appears.

5. Click OK to accept your choice.

You can also use a shortcut method to select a graph type while working in Microsoft Graph. Click the down arrow just to the right of the Chart Type button on the Standard toolbar in Graph. A small palette appears, allowing you to choose from the most commonly used graph types.

Labeling a graph

After you add a graph to your slide, you need to complete the graph by adding labels: a title, labels for the axes, and a deciphering legend. The datasheet only allows you to type in names for column and row labels — you'll have to add the other labels to the graph itself. Add labels to your graph as follows:

1. Double-click your graph to activate the Microsoft Graph program. If you're already working in Microsoft Graph, just single-click your graph to select it.

2. Choose Chart⇨Chart Options from the Menu bar to open the Chart Options dialog box.

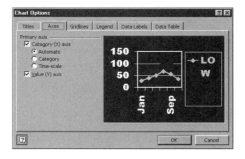

This dialog box offers the following options:

- **Titles:** Add a title for the graph and titles for the axes. To adjust the font and size of a title, exit Chart Options by clicking Cancel in the Chart Options dialog box, click the title that you want to change, and then choose Format⇨Font to make your adjustments.

- **Axes:** Hide or show the labels you gave the data on the datasheet.

• **Gridlines:** Activate and deactivate the horizontal and vertical gridlines lines that appear with the graph. Using this function may help your audience better visualize the position of the plotted data.

• **Legend:** Click the <u>S</u>how legend check box to include a legend on your graph. Also click a radio button to position the legend in the Botto<u>m</u>, C<u>o</u>rner, <u>T</u>op, <u>R</u>ight, or <u>L</u>eft of the graph. To edit the legend, exit the Chart Options dialog box. Double-click the legend on the graph to summon the Format Legend dialog box where you can edit the text and colors of your legend entries.

• **Data Labels:** Display the actual numerical data for each data point in your datasheet on the graph itself. With few exceptions, choose None for displaying labels — the extra text makes the graph appear messy.

• **Data Table:** If you want to show actual data, choose the Data Table option as an accompaniment for your graph. This causes the datasheet from which the graph is constructed to be displayed.

Close the Chart Options dialog box and click your slide (outside the graph) to view your completed graph.

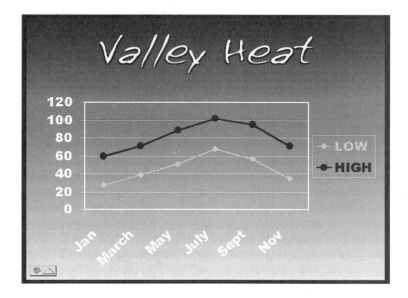

While working on your graph, you can double-click any element — axes labels, datapoints, gridlines, and so on — to open a dialog box that offers you extensive customizing options for that element. These dialog boxes provide you with complete control over the color, size, and other formatting attributes of every element in your graph.

Moving and resizing a graph

Because Microsoft Graph may or may not position your newly created graph in the appropriate location, you may want to move or resize your graph:

✦ **To move a graph:** Click and drag the graph — not on the sizing handles — to move it to a new destination.

✦ **To resize a graph:** Click the graph and then pull on one of its handles. Holding down the Shift key as you resize the graph maintains the proportions of the graph. Be aware that resizing may alter text readability.

Importing Worksheets and Charts from Excel

When you want to include a more detailed worksheet or graph on your PowerPoint slide, you can choose to insert a Microsoft Excel Chart. Excel offers you greater data manipulation and graphing capabilities than Microsoft Graph.

Inserting a Microsoft Excel Chart adds a graph to your slide and provides you with a companion worksheet so you can type in data from which the graph is constructed (similarly to the way Microsoft Graph constructs a graph from the datasheet).

You can switch back and forth between entering data on your worksheet page and displaying your data graphically on the graph page. You can also choose to display either the worksheet page or the graph on your slide.

Insert an Excel Chart as follows:

1. Move to the slide where you want to add an Excel Chart.

2. From the Menu bar, choose Insert⇨Object to summon the Insert Object dialog box.

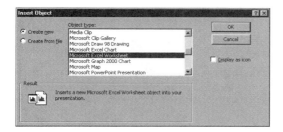

3. In the Object type area, choose Microsoft Excel Chart. Choosing Microsoft Excel Chart causes a little Excel graph to appear on your slide, with a companion worksheet page located on a tab marked Sheet1.

4. Click the tab in the Excel area marked Sheet1 to switch to the Excel worksheet.

5. Fill and manipulate the worksheet cells using standard Excel procedures. Switch to view the graph of your worksheet data at any time by clicking the Chart 1 tab in the Excel area.

6. Click outside the Excel area to return to your slide. Exiting Excel when the worksheet is displayed adds the worksheet to your slide. Exiting Excel when the graph is displayed adds the graph to your slide.

You can reopen and manipulate your worksheet or graph at any time by double-clicking the Excel Worksheet or Chart on your slide. Save your work by choosing File⇨Save from the Menu bar.

Incorporating Organizational Charts

What company doesn't show at least one organizational chart during its monthly all-hands meeting? After all, how would you know who's who in the chain of command . . . who you report to, who reports to you, and who to ignore altogether because they're not even in your department? And what history teacher hasn't spent a least one day mapping out the lineage of some nation's royal family to show who married whom and the names of their resulting offspring?

To show the relationship among several entities without whipping out index cards and strands of yarn and creating your own little pin-up organizational chart, call on PowerPoint and one of its handy little subprograms: Microsoft Organization Chart.

Adding a new slide with an organizational chart

If you know you want an organizational chart on your slide from the get-go, follow these steps:

1. In Slide view, Normal view, or Slide Sorter view, move to the location in your presentation where you want to insert a new slide with an organizational chart.

2. Choose Insert⇨New Slide from the Menu bar, click the New Slide button on the Standard Toolbar, or press Ctrl+M. The New Slide dialog box appears and asks you to choose an AutoLayout.

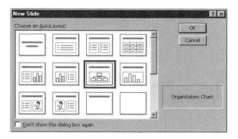

3. In the New Slide dialog box, select an AutoLayout design that includes an organizational chart and click OK. A new slide appears with a placeholder for an organizational chart.

4. Double-click the organizational chart placeholder to begin building your organizational chart. The program creates a sample chart that acts as a template as you construct your own organizational chart.

5. Add your own information to the organizational chart. *See also* "Working with Organization Chart boxes and connectors" later in this section for more details.

6. Choose File➪Exit and Return to go back to the slide. You can also close the Organizational chart window by clicking the X in the upper-right corner.

7. Click Yes when the program asks whether you want to update the object before proceeding. The chart is redrawn with the information you supplied.

Adding an organizational chart to your slide

To add an organizational chart to a slide already in your presentation

1. Move to the slide where you want to add an organizational chart.

2. Choose Insert➪Picture➪Organization Chart from the Menu bar to place a sample organizational chart on your slide.

3. Replace the data in the sample organizational chart with your actual information. *See also* "Working with Organization Chart boxes and connectors" later in this section for more details.

4. Return to the slide by choosing File➪Exit and Return or by clicking the X in the upper-right corner of the Organization Chart window.

5. Click Yes when the program asks you whether you want to update the organizational chart object. The chart is redrawn with the data you input to the datasheet.

Working with Organization Chart boxes and connectors

Microsoft Organization Chart offers you a toolbar that appears just below the Menu bar with a variety of box/connector styles to show the relationship among different entities.

Click a button on the Chart toolbar to choose a box/connector style. Your pointer will turn into a miniature box with your chosen box/connector style. Then click a box in your organization chart to attach it to the new box of your chosen style. The following list gives the skinny on what's available:

✦ **Manager:** A top-level box.

✦ **Subordinate:** A box representing a person who reports to a manager.

✦ **Co-worker:** Anyone who works in a peer relationship with another worker. Co-worker boxes can represent subordinates who report to different managers.

✦ **Assistant:** The assistant's box connects to the box of the person he or she is assisting.

✦ **Group:** Includes all the boxes reporting to a manager.

✦ **Connecting line:** The line that attaches two boxes.

Adding and deleting boxes in an organizational chart

To add a new box to your organizational chart

1. Select the toolbar below the Organizational Chart menu and click the type of box (Manager, Subordinate, and so on) that you want to add.

2. Click the box in your organizational chart that you want to attach the new box to. The new box appears as soon as you click the old one.

3. Fill in the text of your new box, pressing Enter to start each new line.

4. Click outside the new box.

To delete a box from your organizational chart

1. Click the box that you want to delete.

2. Press the Delete key or choose Edit⇨Clear from the Menu bar.

Choosing a group style

The group style of your organizational chart defines how your boxes are positioned relative to one another — kind of like planning the seating arrangement for a holiday dinner.

Choosing a group style can be useful in helping arrange an organizational chart to neatly fit the confined area of a PowerPoint slide. For example, a group style can indicate whether a group of co-worker boxes is arranged horizontally or vertically. An existing group style can also be changed by selecting a group of boxes on the organizational chart and applying a new group style.

You can also employ several group styles within the same chart so that each branch of the chart can be custom-tailored to your needs.

Apply a group style to your chart as follows:

1. Hold down the Shift key as you click each box that you want to include in the new group style. If you want to include the entire chart in the new group style, choose Edit⌦Select⌦All or press Ctrl+A.

2. Select the Styles menu in the Organizational Chart Menu bar and choose a group style from the drop-down list. A miniature of how each style looks is shown in the list. The group style is applied to the boxes you selected.

If you don't like what you've done, just choose Edit⌦Undo Chart Style from the Microsoft Organization Chart Menu bar or press Ctrl+Z.

Moving boxes on an organizational chart

To move a box from one position in a chart to another, just click the box you want to move and drag it to its new location. When you release the box, it automatically appears in its new location. Any grouped boxes move along with it.

Formatting an organizational chart

As a finishing touch for your organizational chart, you may want to color certain boxes, make a few connecting lines thicker, or alter the font and text size to improve readability. Format boxed material presented in your organizational chart as follows:

1. Click the box that you want to format. To format multiple boxes, hold down the Shift key as you click each box. To format all boxes in the chart, choose Edit⌦Select⌦All or press Ctrl+A.

2. Select the Text menu and choose a formatting option (font, color, or alignment of the text in the boxes).

3. Choose the Boxes menu and select a formatting option for the boxes (color, shadow, border style, border color, and border line style of the selected boxes).

You can format the background color of your organizational chart by choosing Chart⌦Background Color and clicking a color in the palette.

Format connecting lines of your organizational chart as follows:

1. Click the connecting line that you want to format. To format multiple connecting lines, hold down the Shift key as you click each line. To format all connecting lines in the chart, choose Edit⇨Select⇨Connecting Lines.

2. Choose the Lines menu and select a formatting option (thickness, style, or color of your chosen connecting lines).

3. When you are done formatting your organization chart, click the X in the upper-right corner to close the Microsoft Organization Chart window. A message appears asking whether you want to update the chart before proceeding. Click Yes to accept your changes. Your completed organization chart appears on your slide.

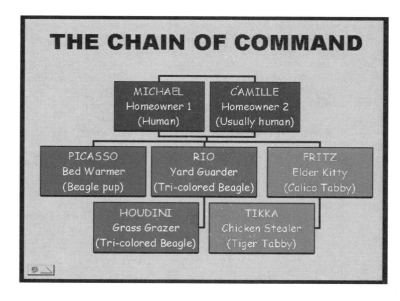

Move the chart by clicking and dragging it to a new location. Resize the chart by pulling on its sizing handles. Edit the chart by double-clicking it to reopen the Microsoft Organization Chart program.

Making Equations with Equation Editor

Equation Editor is a nifty little program that makes generating superscripts, square roots, absolute values, summations, and a whole slew of other mathematical symbols a (fairly) simple task.

Note: This program ships with Microsoft Office. It's probably already installed on your system, but if not, insert your Microsoft Office CD-ROM and choose Start⇨Settings⇨Control Panel⇨ Add/Remove Programs. From the Office Setup screen, proceed with installing the Equation Editor. For more details on installing new programs, please see *Windows 98 For Dummies Quick Reference,* by Greg Harvey, published by IDG Books Worldwide, Inc.

To slap an equation on a slide, follow these steps:

1. In Slide view or Normal view, move to the slide where you want to add an equation.

2. Choose Insert⇨Object to bring up the Insert Object dialog box.

3. Choose Microsoft Equation 3.0 (you may have to scroll down through the list) and click OK. The Equation Editor window appears.

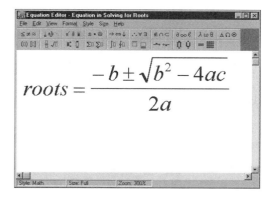

4. Type your equation, using the keyboard keys and the buttons on the Equation toolbar (at the top of the window). This step is easier said than done — you may have to tinker a bit.

If necessary, use the Style menu to format the type of numerical characters in your equation. Style options consist of Math, Text, Function, Variable, Greek, Symbol, and Matrix-Vector. Equation Editor normally performs this formatting task for you because it presents you with preformatted templates you can use. You may occasionally need to adjust the look of your creation so that it conveys the intended mathematical meaning.

5. Choose File⇨Exit and Return to close Equation Editor and add the equation to your slide.

6. Drag the handles of the newly added equation to adjust its size on your slide.

You may also want to change the background color of the equation (or the slide itself) to make the equation easier to read. *See also* Part III for additional information on changing background colors.

To edit an equation on a slide, simply double-click the equation to restart the Equation Editor program. Make your changes and then choose File⇨Exit and Return to return to PowerPoint.

Recording and Printing Meeting Minutes and Action Items

During a slide show, you have the option of recording minutes, action items, audience comments, and brainstorming ideas directly in your PowerPoint presentation. PowerPoint's Meeting Minder function makes it all possible.

Meeting Minder displays all the action items on a new slide at the end of your slide show, providing you and your audience with a concise "to-do" list at the end of your presentation. Minutes and action items can be saved in a new Word document for later editing, printing, and distribution.

Taking notes and minutes during a slide show

Follow these steps to jot down notes or other written records during your presentation:

1. In Slide Show view, right-click the mouse at any time and select Meeting Minder or Speaker Notes. A Meeting Minder dialog box or Speaker Notes dialog box appears accordingly.

Meeting Minder allows you to record meeting minutes and assign action items. Speaker Notes allows you to record notes which are transferred to the Notes Pane of each slide — a good way to tie specific notes to specific slides.

2. Click in the appropriate dialog box and type your minutes or notes. The Meeting Minder dialog box offers two tabs: a Meeting Minutes tab and an Action Items tab. The Action Items tab provides three boxes for you to fill in: Description (of the action item), Assigned To, and Due Date. Another box shows a running list of previous action items you recorded.

The Speaker Notes dialog box provides one blank area for you to type your notes.

3. Click OK to close the Meeting Minder dialog box. Click Close to close the Speaker Notes dialog box.

PowerPoint 2000 users convening in an online meeting can use the Meeting Minder dialog box and the Speaker Notes dialog box to take records. Notes taken can be viewed by everyone taking part in the meeting. *See also* Part IX for additional information.

Saving meeting minutes and action items to a Word document

Suppose you want to save and print meeting minutes and action items as a Word document for easy archiving and distribution. You're in luck! Just follow these steps:

1. Working in Slide Show view, right-click the mouse, select Meeting Minder, and click the Meeting Minutes or Action Items tab.

2. Type to record minutes or action items throughout the meeting. *See also* "Taking notes and minutes during a slide show," earlier in this section for more details.

3. Click Export, and the Meeting Minder Export dialog box appears.

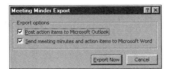

4. Click to check the Send meeting minutes and action items to Microsoft Word check box (if it isn't already checked) and click Export Now.

Microsoft Word opens and copies the exported Meeting Minder contents to a new document. You can now save and print your document using standard Word functions.

Sending a list of action items to Outlook

It's a good idea to have Microsoft Outlook installed on the system where you're showing your PowerPoint presentation. Why? Because if you do, you can send action items recorded in the Meeting Minder to Outlook for task assignment to the responsible individuals by following these steps:

1. Working in Slide Show view, right-click the mouse, select Meeting Minder to make the Meeting Minder dialog box appear.

2. Click the Action Items tab.

3. Click Export. The Meeting Minder Export dialog box appears.

4. Click to check the Post action items to Microsoft Outlook check box (if it isn't already checked) and click Export Now.

Recorded action items are posted to your task list in Outlook. Tasks can then be assigned and marked for follow-up and completion.

During a presentation, you can click the Schedule button in the Meeting Minder dialog box to set up a meeting in Outlook. But again, Outlook must be installed on the system where you show your presentation.

Using Tables

Inserting massive quantities of text on your PowerPoint slides is rarely a good idea. Too many words means you have to use a small text point size to fit everything in, which may make it difficult for audience members to read your slides.

If you're forced to present text-intensive information, consider organizing that information into a tidy table.

Inserting a new slide with a table

The easiest way to insert a simple table on a PowerPoint slide is to create a new slide with a table placeholder:

1. In Slide view, Normal view, or Slide Sorter view, move to the location in your presentation where you want to insert a new slide with a table.

2. Choose Insert⇨New Slide from the Menu bar, click the New Slide button on the Standard toolbar, or press Ctrl+M.

3. In the New Slide dialog box, select the Table AutoLayout and click OK.

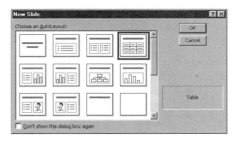

4. In Slide view or Normal view, double-click the table placeholder. The Insert Table dialog box appears.

5. Type the desired number of columns and rows in the Insert Table dialog box and then click OK.

6. Type and format text in each cell just as you do in a text box.

7. Click outside the table to return to your slide. You can resize your new table by clicking and dragging any of its handles.

Inserting a simple table on an existing slide

You can add a simple table to any existing slide by following these steps:

1. In Slide view or Normal view, move to the Slide where you want to insert a simple table.

 2. Click the Insert Table button on the Standard toolbar.

3. Hold the mouse button down and drag the mouse to select the number of rows and columns you want. Release the mouse button to accept your chosen dimensions.

4. Type and format text in each cell, just as you do in a text box.

5. Click outside the table to return to your slide. You can resize your new table by clicking and dragging any of its handles.

Formatting a simple table

Several tools exist to help you in formatting your simple table (if you are not already editing the table, click the table once to start editing):

✦ **To resize row height or column width:** Click and drag a line that defines the border of the row or column.

✦ **To insert a new row (or column):** Highlight the row (column) where you want to insert the new row (column). Right-click the mouse and choose Insert Rows (Insert Columns). A new row appears above the selected row; a new column appears to the left of the selected column.

✦ **To delete a row (or column):** Select the row (column) to be deleted. Right-click the mouse and choose Delete Rows (Delete Columns).

✦ **To format the borders, fill, text orientation, and other attributes:** Select the cells to be formatted. Right-click the mouse and choose Borders and Fill. The Format Table dialog box appears. The Format Table dialog box offers three tabs — Borders, Fill, and Text Box — that help you adjust table formatting.

Right-click outside the simple table to stop editing and return to the slide. Click and drag your simple table to move it to a new location on the slide. Resize your simple table by pulling on the sizing handles.

Inserting a Word table on an existing slide

If you're already an expert tablemaker using Microsoft Word, you can save yourself a significant amount of effort by building your table in Word:

1. In Slide view or Normal view, move to the slide where you want to add a table.

2. On the Standard toolbar, choose Insert⇨Picture⇨Microsoft Word Table.

3. Type a number in the Number of Columns and the Number of Rows areas in the Insert Table dialog box. A blank table appears with your chosen number of columns and rows.

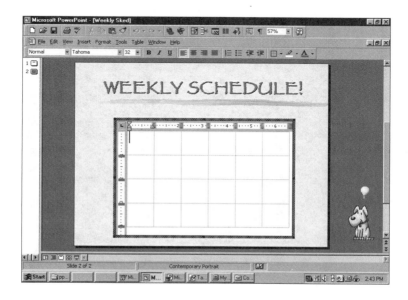

4. Fill the table cells and adjust text formatting and cell formatting using standard Word table procedures. You can also right-click the mouse to check out additional table formatting options.

Table text is not visible in the outline pane of your PowerPoint presentation.

5. Click outside the table to complete its creation and return to PowerPoint. Your newly created table appears on the slide.

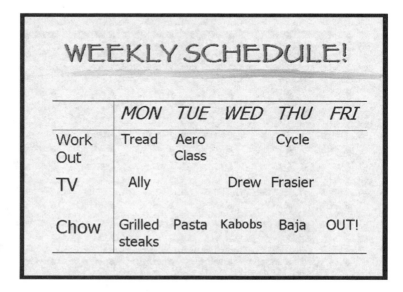

	MON	TUE	WED	THU	FRI
Work Out	Tread	Aero Class		Cycle	
TV	Ally		Drew	Frasier	
Chow	Grilled steaks	Pasta	Kabobs	Baja	OUT!

WEEKLY SCHEDULE!

Click and drag your table to reposition where it sits on the slide.

 You can edit a completed table at any time by double-clicking the table and using the Word tools and menus to make modifications.

Working with Speaker Notes

Notes are like little speaker cue cards, perfect for reminding you to tell a joke, make eye contact, or pause contemplatively. You can add notes to every page of your presentation. I use them frequently to explain at great length the cursory bullet items I use on-screen.

The notes don't appear during the slide show presentation itself. Most importantly, you can print the notes and use them at the podium to remind you of what to say during the real deal.

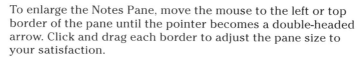
In Normal, Slide, and Outline view

Follow these steps to add notes to the Notes Pane in Normal, Slide, and Outline view:

1. Move to the slide to which you want to add notes.

2. Click the Notes Pane, located in the lower-right corner of the screen, and then type your notes for the current slide.

To enlarge the Notes Pane, move the mouse to the left or top border of the pane until the pointer becomes a double-headed arrow. Click and drag each border to adjust the pane size to your satisfaction.

In Notes Page view

Notes Page view is a special view that shows each slide and the slide's speaker notes on a separate page of paper. When you look at a page in Notes Page view, you see a slide thumbnail at the top of the page, and your speaker notes in a text box at the bottom of the page.

You use Notes Pages view to print your speaker notes. The print outs you create in this view are really intended for use by a speaker in delivering a presentation — not for distribution as handouts to the audience. *See also* Part VIII for the details on creating handouts.

Only one slide is visible per page. Each Notes Page is viewed individually, and you can move between pages by using the same procedures for moving between slides.

Switch to Notes Page view by choosing View➪Notes Page from the Menu bar.

Follow these steps to add notes to the notes area in Notes Page view:

1. Move to the slide where you want to add speaker notes.

2. Click the notes area (inside the text box) and begin typing. The text box in the notes area of Notes Page view allows you to type and format your speaker notes in the same fashion you would in any word-processing document. You can change text fonts, sizes, and colors and add bullets or numbers.

Just in case you're the wordy type and you run out of room for your notes on a slide in Notes Page view, you have a few options for increasing notes space:

✦ **Increase the size of the text box in the notes area of Notes Page view:** Grab a handle at the top of the text box and stretch upwards to resize the box. You probably need to shrink the size of the slide thumbnail: click the slide, grab a handle, and resize as needed to make room for the expanding text box. This changes only the current page. If you want to increase the size of the notes text box for all the pages, you need to make adjustments to the Notes Master. *See also* Part III for details on editing the Notes Master.

✦ **Delete the slide thumbnail on the current slide:** If you're a real space hog, you can just click and delete the slide placeholder at the top of the notes page. This doesn't delete the slide itself — just its placeholder on the notes page. It will be up to you to remember what slide the current notes are associated with!

Part VII

Showing Your Presentation

PowerPoint offers some great features to help you motivate through the presentation of your slide show. This part tells you how to polish off that presentation and get on with the show!

In this part . . .

✔ **Using action buttons in your presentation**

✔ **Adding cool transitions to your slides**

✔ **Setting up and showing your presentation**

Adding Action Buttons

PowerPoint 2000 offers you some way-cool *action buttons* that you can click during a slide show to perform certain specialized functions. You can use action buttons to perform a range of functions, such as running external programs or moving to certain slides.

The process of adding an action button to a slide involves first creating the button itself, then defining its function. To add an action button to a slide, follow these steps:

1. In Normal or Slide view, move to the slide where you want to add an action button.

2. Choose AutoShapes⇨Action Buttons from the Drawing toolbar to bring up the Action Buttons toolbox.

3. In the Action Buttons toolbox, click a button shape. You can choose buttons that represent actions, such as home, forward, backward, document, and movie. You can embellish the blank button with text to customize your choices (*see also* Step 6).

4. Click your slide to start drawing the button, starting with the upper-left corner of the button. Drag the mouse until the button reaches the size that you want; then release the mouse button. An Action Settings dialog box appears.

5. In the Action Settings dialog box click the Mouse Click or Mouse Over tab. Choosing Mouse Click requires that you click the button in order to execute its action, while choosing Mouse Over requires only that you move the mouse on top of the button (without clicking) to perform the button action.

6. Assign an action to your newly created button. Default actions are preset for many buttons. For example, returning to the home slide (the first slide in the presentation) is the default action for the action button that looks like a house.

TIP

To find out the default action of a button, consult the Hyperlink to area of the Action Settings dialog box.

You may want to redefine button actions according to your specific needs. Use the following options in the Action Settings dialog box to redefine button actions:

- **None:** No action is taken.

- **Hyperlink to:** Activates a drop-down list indicating everywhere the hyperlink can go. *See* Part IX for more information on hyperlinks.

- **Run program:** Allows you to choose a program that runs when you click the action button. *Note:* If you choose this option, you need to be certain that the program is available on whatever system you run your presentation.

- **Run macro:** Produces a list of all available macros in the presentation. *See also* Part X for details on macros.

- **Object action:** Applies to a slide object to which you can assign the action of open, play, or edit. For example, you can assign the play action to a movie clip, or assign the open or edit action to an Excel Chart. To use this option, switch to Slide view or Normal view and click the object you want to attach an action to. Right-click the object and choose Action Settings from the menu. On the Mouse Click or Mouse Over tab, click the Object action radio button and choose Open, Play, or Edit from the drop-down list.

- **Play sound:** Plays a sound in conjunction with any other action taken. You can choose from sounds in PowerPoint's Clip Gallery or your own files. A neat idea is to play a cash register sound when you click a button that links to an Excel financial spreadsheet. *See also* Part V for details on sounds.

- **Highlight click:** Applies to an object other than an action button to which you attach an action. Because action buttons highlight when clicked or moused over, checking this option allows other objects — like movies or text boxes — to look as if they, too, are being clicked or moused over.

After you have made your selections, click OK to close the Action Settings dialog box.

7. (Optional) Tweak the button's appearance: Pull the handles to adjust the button size and yank on the diamond handle to alter the 3-D effect of the button. Move the entire button by clicking it and dragging it to another place on your slide. Adjust the fill color as you do for any drawing object. *See also* Part V for details.

You can add text to any selected button by right-clicking the action button, choosing Add Text, and then typing at the cursor. Button text can be formatted using the Formatting toolbar.

Button text looks best on blank buttons.

If you want to change a button's action setting at a later time, right-click the action button and select the Action Settings command from the menu.

Adding Slide Transitions

Slide transitions dictate how slides enter and exit as you present your slide show.

You can opt to use one type of transition consistently throughout your entire presentation, or you can choose unique transitions for individual slides. You can also adjust the speed at which a transition occurs — slow, medium, or fast — and even have a sound play as the transition takes place.

PowerPoint provides you with more than 40 cool transitions to use in your presentations. (Personally, I really like the Cover and Uncover transitions.) You can add transitions to your presentation using either the Slide Transition Effects menu or the Slide Transition dialog box. Creating transitions with the menu is the more expedient process, while creating transitions with the dialog box allows you greater control over transition details like speed and sound.

Adding a transition to a slide dictates how that slide will enter on-screen — not how it will exit. PowerPoint doesn't allow you to set up an exit transition.

Using the Slide Transition Effects menu

To add transitions to your presentation using the Slide Transition Effects menu, follow these steps:

1. In Slide Sorter view, click on a slide where you want to add a transition. To select multiple slides, hold down Shift as you click. To select all slides, choose Edit➪Select All or press Ctrl+A.

2. Click the down arrow tab on the Slide Transition Effects menu and select a transition. PowerPoint tags each slide with a transition effects marker indicating that a transition has been added.

In Slide Sorter view, clicking a slide's transition effects tag causes a thumbnail preview of the transition to play.

Using the Slide Transition dialog box

To add transitions to your presentation using the Slide Transition dialog box

1. In any view except Slide Show view, click on a slide where you want to add a transition. To select multiple slides in Slide Sorter view, hold down Shift as you click. To select all slides in either view, choose Edit➪Select All or press Ctrl+A.

2. Choose Slide Show➪Slide Transition from the Menu bar. The Slide Transition dialog box appears.

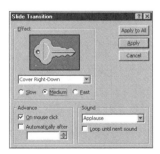

3. In the Effect area of the Slide Transition dialog box, choose a transition from the drop-down menu box. Also choose a transition speed: Slow, Medium, or Fast. A thumbnail preview shows how your choices appear in the slide show.

4. In the Advance area, choose whether you want the transition to occur On mouse click or Automatically after. Choosing Automatically after allows you to specify the number of seconds before the transition is performed. You have the option of leaving the number of seconds a 0 — the default — which causes each transition to play directly after the previous transition finishes.

5. If you want a sound to accompany your transition, select a sound from the drop-down menu box in the Sound area (choose Other Sound to use non-PowerPoint sound files). The Loop until next sound option causes the sound to play repeatedly until another sound in the presentation is played.

6. Click Apply to accept and apply your choices or click Apply to All if you want your choices applied to every slide in the presentation.

PowerPoint allows you to apply any transition to any slide. However, if you want to look like a real PowerPoint pro, I encourage you to pick one transition type and apply it consistently throughout your entire presentation. Don't use any transition with the adjective *random* in its name. Be creative, but don't overdo it, because then your audience pays more attention to your wacky transitions than to the information on your slides. You appear most professional if you choose something elegant, like a straight cut (the No Transition choice), a Fade Through Black, or a Dissolve, Cover, Uncover, Wipe, or Strip. Avoid the Blind and Checkerboard effects — they will totally annoy your audience!

For those of you delivering your presentations over compressed video technologies — like desktop video — don't bother with transitions at all. Compression often obliterates the motion of a transition.

Showing Your Slides via Computer

After creating your presentation, you're ready to take your message to the world. PowerPoint allows you lots of control over your presentation when you deliver it on your computer — or via other low-tech options. *See* "Low-tech options" later in this part to read about different ways to present your slide show without a computer.

Preparing your show for presentation

After you create your slides, you have to make some final decisions about how your show will be presented.

1. Choose Slide Show➪Set Up Show from the Menu bar. The Set Up Show dialog box appears.

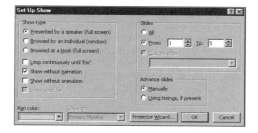

2. Click one of the following three radio buttons in the Show type section:

   • **Presented by a speaker:** Sets up a full-screen presentation in which a speaker controls how the show is presented — including taking meeting minutes and recording action items. The speaker controls the pace of the presentation by clicking through slides at his or her own pace.

   • **Browsed by an individual:** Sets up a smaller screen presentation, which appears in its own window with commands for navigating the show and for editing and printing slides. Other files can be open on-screen at the same time. This option is most frequently used by someone who browses the show over a company intranet.

   • **Browsed at a kiosk:** Creates a full-screen self-running presentation that is most often used in an unattended display at a convention or a mall. The show restarts after 5 minutes of inactivity. Navigation commands (hyperlinks and action buttons) can be included to give users perusing the show control over how they view the presentation — but users can't modify the presentation itself.

3. Click one or more of the following three check boxes:

   • **Loop continuously until 'Esc':** Starts over at the first slide after the show finishes, until the presenter or user presses the Esc key.

   • **Show without narration:** Checking this option allows you to turn off narration that you record using the Record Narration option on the Slide Show menu. This option allows you to present face-to-face a slide show that's typically presented without a speaker (for example, a self-running show at a kiosk).

- **Show without animation:** Shows each slide in its final form, as if all animations have been performed. Check this option to show an animation-free version of your presentation. Showing your slide show without animations speeds up the presentation. This is an important option to have available when the half-hour of presentation time you were told you'd have has suddenly been reduced to ten minutes.

If you previously selected Browsed by an individual, you can also check the Show Scrollbar box. This option places a scrollbar on the slide show window to make all parts of the window accessible to the person viewing the show.

4. Choose to show All the slides in the presentation or specify a range in the From and To boxes. You may also choose to present a Custom Show you created from your presentation. Click the tab to reveal a drop-down menu of Custom Shows available. The Custom Show tab is deselected if you have no Custom Shows. *See also* "Creating Custom Shows" later in this section for more information.

5. Choose whether the presenter or user Manually proceeds from slide to slide or whether the slides should advance Using timings, if present. *See also* "Automating the slide show with slide timings" later in this section.

6. (Optional) If you plan to use the pen during your presentation, accept the default color for the pen tool, or get a little crazy and change to some other color. *See also* "Writing with the slide show pen" later in this section.

7. (Optional) Choose a monitor on which to present your slide show to an audience. This function allows you to run the slide show on two screens simultaneously — one with full-screen slides for the audience, and the other with notes and outline panes for you (the presenter). You only get this option on systems running Windows 98 or Windows 2000, with dual-monitor hardware configured.

Clicking the Projector Wizard button brings up a wizard that assists you in setting up the projection system — the computer projection system — for your show. Note that a computer projector is not the same as an overhead projector! A computer projector is a high-tech (and relatively expensive) system that connects to your computer and beams your computer display through a high-powered lens onto a large screen. An overhead projector is the familiar device from high school that your algebra teacher used to show overhead transparencies. *See also* "Computer projectors" later in this part for more information.

It's always a good idea to choose the <u>L</u>oop continuously until 'Esc' option. If you choose this option, you return to your first slide when you complete your presentation. Without looping, your audience ends up staring at an ugly old slide construction view (whatever you started the show from — for example, from Slide Sorter view) when you click off your final slide. If you choose the <u>B</u>rowsed by an individual option and don't loop back, the viewer sees the words "End of slide show, click to exit" after the last slide.

Presenting slide shows manually

If you choose to run your show manually (see the preceding section for your other options), move to the first slide in your presentation and do one of the following to start the show:

✦ Choose Sli<u>d</u>e Show⇨<u>V</u>iew Show from the Menu bar.

 ✦ Click the Slide Show button from the row of view buttons in the lower-left corner of the PowerPoint window.

✦ Press F5.

Besides speaking eloquently and making eye-contact with your audience members, you spend the majority of your time delivering a manually run PowerPoint slide show performing the following tasks:

✦ **Moving along:** The first slide of your show appears and stays on-screen until you click the left mouse button.

If you created animation that builds your slide one bullet at a time, only the unanimated objects appear at the start of each slide. Click the mouse button to show the first animation and continue clicking to advance each additional animation. When all animations on a slide are complete, click the mouse button to move to the next slide.

✦ **Writing notes on the slides:** Make notes on a slide by picking up the pen and holding down the left mouse button as you write. Release the button to stop writing. *See* "Writing with the slide show pen" later in this part for more information on using the pen.

Use the following shortcuts to perform any of these other slick presentation tasks.

To Do This	Perform This Action
Show Actions menu	Right-click
Advance to next animation or next slide	Left-click, press spacebar, right arrow, down arrow, or N
Back up one animation or slide	Press Backspace, left arrow, up arrow, or P
Show specific slide	Press slide number and then press Enter
Toggle screen black (to direct audience attention away from the slide show)	Press B
Toggle screen white (to direct audience attention away from the slide show)	Press W
Show/hide pointer	Press A or =
Change arrow to pen	Press Ctrl+P
Change pen to arrow	Press Ctrl+A
Erase screen doodles	Press E
End slide show	Press Esc

 A handful of other keyboard sequences yield certain bizarre results during your slide show. Don't get too curious about these other shortcuts during a really important presentation to the board of directors.

Automating the slide show with slide timings

Use slide timings whenever you want to create a stand-alone show. This option allows you to designate how long each slide appears on-screen before the next slide appears.

To set the slide timings

1. Choose Slide Show⇔Rehearse Timings from the Menu bar.
   The show starts and a small Rehearsal dialog box with a timer appears in the corner of the screen. The Rehearsal dialog box times how long each slide is displayed, as well as the total time for the entire presentation. PowerPoint displays both times in the dialog box.

2. Display Slide 1 for whatever duration you choose; left-click to advance to the next animation or next slide.

When you click to Slide 2, PowerPoint records how long you displayed Slide 1. PowerPoint resets the timer to zero to start recording how long Slide 2 is displayed.

If you mess up timing a slide, click the Repeat button in the Rehearsal dialog box and try timing the slide again. Clicking the Pause button in the Rehearsal dialog box pauses the timing process. Resume timing by pressing Pause again.

3. Continue clicking to advance your slides until you reach the end of the show. PowerPoint times how long each slide is displayed. It also times how long the entire show runs from start to finish.

4. After you time the last slide, PowerPoint informs you of the total time for the show and asks whether you want to record the presentation as timed. Click Yes to accept your timings or No to ditch them.

Set the show to run with timings by clicking the Using timings, if present radio button in the Set Up Show dialog box (*see also* "Preparing your show for presentation" earlier in this part). Now you can play hooky while PowerPoint does all the work!

Writing with the slide show pen

The slide show pen is a handy resource for pointing out key text or important items on a slide during your presentation. It serves the same purpose as a laser pointer, except that the marks created by the pen stay on the slide until you move to another slide in the slide show.

Notes aren't permanent! If you leave a slide and then return, the notes vanish. So don't write anything important with the pen. Instead, make notes you intend to keep in the Meeting Minder or Speaker Notes dialog boxes. *See* Part VI for more information on using the Meeting Minder or Speaker Notes dialog boxes.

Keep these points in mind when you use the pen during your presentation:

✦ To "pick up" the pen during a show, press Ctrl+P or right-click the mouse and choose Pointer Options⇨Pen in the menu.

✦ Write on the slide by clicking and holding the left mouse button while you simultaneously move the mouse as if it were a writing utensil. After writing on a slide, you need to press Ctrl+A or right-click and choose Pointer Options⇨Arrow to continue navigating your presentation.

✦ You can hide the slide show pen or pointer during a slide show by right-clicking the mouse and choosing Pointer Options➪Hidden. Retrieve a hidden pointer or pen during the slide show by right-clicking the mouse and choosing Pointer Options➪Automatic.

The writing color of the pen is preset to coordinate with the color scheme of your slides, but this color can be changed at any time to suit your own personal taste. To change the pen color prior to starting a slide show, choose Slide Show➪Set Up Show from the Menu bar. Click your choice of color in the Pen Color box. To change the pen color during a slide show, right-click the mouse, choose Pointer Options➪Pen Color, and pick a new color.

Creating Custom Shows

PowerPoint Custom Shows allow you to create multiple, customized presentations from a single slide show. Instead of building entirely separate — but similar — presentations for unique audience groupings, PowerPoint lets you pick a subset of slides from your presentation and bundle them together as a Custom Show.

For example, you can create a 20-slide presentation for an employee briefing and then customize a 10-slide executive summary subset of the briefing for top-level managers. You can then create a 15-slide Custom Show from the same material for a different audience.

To create a new Custom Show, follow these steps:

1. Choose Slide Show➪Custom Shows from the Menu bar. The Custom Shows dialog box appears and lists any Custom shows that you have already created.

2. In the Custom Shows dialog box, click New. The Define Custom Show dialog box appears.

3. In the Slide show name box, type a name for your Custom Show.

4. In the Slides in presentation box, click a slide that you want to add to your Custom Show and click Add. Repeat for each slide you want to add. Added slides appear in the Slides in custom show box.

5. Click OK to accept your Custom Show. This returns you to the Custom Shows dialog box.

6. Click Close to exit the dialog box.

You can preview your Custom Show by clicking the name of the show in the Custom Shows dialog box and clicking the Show button.

A Custom Show can be edited after it has been created. Add or delete slides from a Custom Show as follows:

1. Choose Slide Show⇨Custom Shows from the Menu bar.

2. In the Custom Shows dialog box, click the name of the Custom Show that you want to edit and click Edit. The Define Custom Show dialog box opens.

- **To add a slide to your Custom Show:** In the Slides in presentation box, click a slide that you want to add to your Custom Show and click Add. Repeat for each slide that you want to add. Added slides appear in the Slides in custom show box.

- **To delete a slide from your Custom Show:** In the Slides in custom show box, click a slide that you want to remove from your Custom Show and click Remove. Removed Slides return to the Slides in presentation box.

- **To reorder slides in the Custom Show:** Click a slide in the Slides in custom show box that you wish to move. Click the up or down arrow in the Define Custom Show dialog box to move the selected slide up or down in the presentation order.

3. Click OK to accept your Custom Show and return to the Custom Shows dialog box.

4. Click Close to exit the dialog box.

To delete an entire Custom Show, click its name in the Custom Shows dialog box and click Remove. Only the Custom Show itself is removed — not the original slides in the presentation.

Presenting without PowerPoint installed

In case you have to give a show without your trusty computer, you want to avoid the possibility (and embarrassment) of reaching the location for your presentation and discovering that PowerPoint isn't installed there. You can't legally copy the PowerPoint program files onto the destination computer — and you wouldn't want to go through the lengthy install process anyway. Your best bet is to use PowerPoint's Pack and Go feature.

Pack and Go neatly bundles your presentation, presentation fonts, and a PowerPoint Viewer onto some form of portable media such as a 3.5-inch diskette, a Zip disk, or a Jaz disk. You can pop your portable media into the destination computer and present your slide show — even though the computer has no PowerPoint! You can also Pack and Go to a local drive and then e-mail your presentation anywhere in the world via the Internet. The recipient of the e-mail can download the attached presentation and use the sent PowerPoint Viewer to run your slide show.

The PowerPoint Viewer that comes with PowerPoint 2000 supports all PowerPoint 97 and PowerPoint 95 features. The Viewer allows you to view files created for both Windows and Macs.

A wizard guides you through the packaging process. Just follow these steps:

1. Open the PowerPoint presentation that you want to take with you.

2. Choose File➪Pack and Go from the Menu bar. The Pack and Go Wizard appears.

3. Follow the wizard screens to completion, specifying a destination disk when prompted.

Use the following tips to guide you as you pack your presentation:

✦ You can pack the Active presentation or Browse to locate Other presentation(s) you want to pack.

✦ The wizard asks which drive you want your packed presentation sent to. You can Pack and Go to a folder on your hard drive or network drive, then worry later about e-mailing the packed presentation somewhere or copying it to some other removable media.

✦ If your slide show is short and mainly composed of text, you can probably fit the whole thing on a 3.5-inch diskette (which most likely goes in your A drive). If your presentation is too big to fit on a single 3.5-inch diskette, the wizard asks you to insert additional diskettes. If your slide show is large or uses lots of pictures, video, or sound, you may have to store its packed file on a Zip or Jaz disk (which most likely go in your F or G drive).

✦ If you want to burn a CD-ROM of your packed presentation, you need to do so as a two-step process: First pack your presentation to your hard drive (or network drive), 3.5-inch diskette, Zip disk, or Jaz disk; then use that packed file as the source file for your CD-writer.

✦ When prompted by the wizard, be sure to include the PowerPoint Viewer with your packed file. This is the little program that makes it possible to play your presentation on computers where PowerPoint is not installed.

✦ Click to place a check in the Include linked files and Embed TrueType fonts check boxes. Clicking the linked files option includes sounds and videos that your slides call upon in your presentation. Clinking the fonts option helps ensure that your presentation shows text in the same fonts from its original construction — even if the destination computer doesn't have those fonts installed.

TrueType fonts with built-in copyright restrictions can't be packed.

Packed Web presentations are unpacked as Microsoft PowerPoint presentations. *See also* Part IX for details about working with PowerPoint on the Web.

If you edit your presentation after you use the Pack and Go Wizard, you need to run the wizard again to incorporate the changes into your packed files.

To run the packed presentation on a destination computer

1. Insert the disk containing the packed program into the drive of the destination computer.

2. Locate the Pngsetup.exe program on the disk. Double-click Pngsetup.exe to run the program. A Pack and Go Setup dialog box appears.

3. Indicate where you want the unpacked program to be copied: on your C drive, your D drive, or somewhere else.

4. Double-click the PowerPoint Viewer icon created by the setup program. The PowerPoint Viewer dialog box appears.

5. Click the presentation that you want to show. A thumbnail of the selected presentation appears in the dialog box.

 The Pack and Go Wizard gives some pretty strange names, such as pres0.ppz, to packed presentations. After packing, you may wish to rename files with their original names.

6. Click <u>S</u>how to start the presentation. All keyboard and mouse shortcuts are activated, just as they operate on a computer with PowerPoint installed.

 The PowerPoint Viewer does not support certain PowerPoint 2000 features, including picture bullets and automatic numbering.

Although the PowerPoint Viewer ships on the PowerPoint 2000 CD-ROM, you can also download the Viewer from the PowerPoint Web site. One reason you may want to do so is that the Web site offers new updates of the Viewer. *See also* Part I for more information about accessing the PowerPoint Office Update Web site.

Using Alternative Presentation Methods

The ultimate goal of creating your slides is, of course, to show them. PowerPoint is at its best when you show your presentations on a computer, but the Microsoft powers-that-be recognize that not everyone finds this method to be the best way to present a slide show. Consequently, PowerPoint offers you a handful of nifty viewing options to display your presentation to your audience.

High-tech options employ the computer and offer flexibility in the way you present your slides. Low-tech options, however, require no computer but limit you somewhat in the methods you use to display slides.

Computer projectors

To run a PowerPoint presentation from a computer and a computer projector, follow these steps:

1. Use an appropriate cable to connect the external display port on the computer to the computer projector input.

2. In PowerPoint, open the presentation you want to display through the computer projector.

3. From the Menu bar, choose Slide Show⇨Set Up Show. In the Set Up Show dialog box, click the Projector Wizard button to make the Projector Wizard appear.

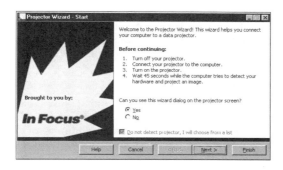

4. Follow the wizard screens to set up and test the video and audio connections for the specific computer projection system you are using.

Scan converters and monitors

A great way to present your PowerPoint presentation to large audiences is through a big-screen television. By using a scan converter to synchronize the computer output and the television signals, you can display a crisp replica of your computer-generated slides on the television screen.

Running your computer display output through a scan converter is also the option of choice for those of you planning to display your slides via closed-circuit TV, satellite, or compressed video.

This option's cost can range from very cheap to very expensive. Be prepared to spend $80 for a low-end scan converter and $2,000 for a spectacular one. Don't forget to also consider the costs associated with purchasing televisions (regular or big screen) for the viewing audiences at each of your receiving sites.

The typical setup is as simple as cabling your computer to a scan converter, the converter to VCR input, and the VCR output to a TV input or antenna. You probably need to select Line In on your VCR and turn the TV to Channel 3 or 4. See the manuals that accompany your purchased scan converter for details.

Many new laptops have an S-video output port that allows you to directly connect your computer to a television, bypassing the need for a scan converter.

LCD panels

A medium-tech option is to send the computer output to an *LCD* panel — a liquid crystal display panel. The LCD panel is a lightweight, portable screen that sits atop an overhead projector. When the overhead projector is turned on, it projects the computer images of the LCD panel onto a white screen. The clarity of the LCD isn't nearly as sharp, however, as other display options.

Low-tech options

For times when you simply have no means of showing your slides through a computer, PowerPoint gives you two low-tech presentation options: overhead transparencies and 35mm slides. *See* Part VIII for details on generating materials for both of these options.

Part VIII

Publishing Your Presentation

PowerPoint allows you to make your presentation available to your audience long after you have finished soliloquizing and mouse-clicking through your presentation. Audience members are likely to want to jot down notes as you speak, and you can come off as the consummate professional by providing your audience with a take-home printout of slides used in your presentation. PowerPoint also ensures your presentation's success with multiple presentation options — including computerless formats like 35mm slides and transparencies — just in case you find yourself operating in a technology-free zone.

In this part . . .

✔ **Printing handouts of PowerPoint slides**

✔ **Presenting with 35mm slides and transparencies**

Creating a Printout of Your Presentation

As in other Microsoft Office programs, the easiest way to print your PowerPoint slides is to click the Print button on the Standard toolbar. This button doesn't bring up any choices or options — it simply prints a single copy of your entire presentation.

To have more options for printing your presentation, you must open the Print dialog box.

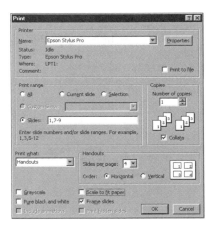

You can open the Print dialog box by using any one of the following methods:

✦ Choose File⇨Print from the Menu bar.

✦ Press Ctrl+P.

✦ Press Ctrl+Shift+F12.

Clicking OK in the Print dialog box without changing any options has the same effect as simply clicking the Print button on the Standard toolbar. However, tweaking the options in the dialog box provides you with greater flexibility in the way you execute the print job. In this dialog box, you can change the following things:

✦ The printer on which your PowerPoint presentation is printed

✦ Which slides are printed

✦ The number of copies that you want to print

✦ What is printed, from slides only to slides with speaker notes

◆ How many slides are printed on a page

◆ Whether slides are printed in color, grayscale, or black and white

The Print dialog box doesn't, however, arrange to load paper when the printer's paper tray runs out.

Changing printers

All available printers — including an option to fax — are listed in the Name field of the Print dialog box. To see the options, click the arrow tab next to the Name field. If you don't see the name of a printer to which you're networked, you need to install that printer's driver before you can use it for a print job.

After you select a printer, click the Properties button to adjust printing properties such as paper size, source tray, graphics resolutions, and page orientation (portrait or landscape). The properties you get to choose from depend on the printer you are using.

Selecting a print range

One of the nifty little attributes of the Print dialog box is the flexibility it gives you in printing out your PowerPoint presentation. For example, if you find a ghastly mistake on a single slide, you don't have to reprint the whole presentation all over again; you can simply correct and reprint the errant slide.

The Print range portion of the Print dialog box gives you the following options when printing your slides:

◆ **All:** Prints the whole presentation — every slide — from start to finish.

◆ **Current slide:** Prints just the slide you're on.

◆ **Selection:** Prints only the slides in the range you select. This option is available only after you highlight slides for printing from the Normal, Slide, Outline, or Slide Sorter views. The advantage? It permits you to print your range without remembering slide numbers in your noodle.

◆ **Custom Show:** Prints a Custom Show you previously saved. *See also* Part VII for more information on creating a Custom Show.

◆ **Slides:** Prints only specific slide numbers and slide ranges of the entire presentation. For example, if you reorder slides 2, 3, and 4, and then find spelling errors on slides 9 and 11, you type 2-4,9,11, with no spaces between characters in the list. Only slides 2, 3, 4, 9, and 11 will be printed.

Selecting the number of copies

The Copies area of the Print dialog box is where you get to think like a photocopier. Use the Number of copies spinner to choose how many copies you want; just click the spinner until your chosen number appears in the box. Also click the check box to choose whether you want to Collate copies or keep copies of the same sheet bundled together. You may want to consider sparing your ink cartridge by printing only one copy and then using a photocopier to do the grunt work of mass duplication.

Specifying what you want printed

The Print what pull-down menu at the bottom of the Print dialog box lets you make a few choices to specify exactly what you want to print, including the following options:

✦ **Slides:** Prints individual slides, one per page. This option is available only when your slides are animation-free.

✦ **Handouts:** Selecting this option activates the Handouts area of the Print dialog box. The Handouts area includes the option of printing two, three, four, six, or nine slides per page for distribution to audience members who wish to forever treasure your memorable presentation. *See also* "Printing Audience Handouts" later in this part.

✦ **Notes Pages:** Prints each slide, one per page, as a small thumbnail followed by a text box comprising notes from the Notes Pane.

✦ **Outline view:** Prints an ordered, text-only outline version of your slides from start to finish. Saves space when you require a printout only of what your slides say and not how your presentation looks.

Choosing more options

The remaining check boxes residing at the bottom of the Print dialog box perform a handful of important functions. Here's what they do:

✦ **Grayscale:** Prints color slides as grayscale slides when printing on a black ink printer.

✦ **Pure black and white:** Prints dark colors, grays, and blacks as black; prints light colors, grays, and whites as white. Works well for text only.

✦ **Include Animations:** On the printout, annotates animations as icons.

+ **Scale to fit paper:** Checks the size of the paper in the printer and reduces or enlarges the size of the slides to fill the printed page.

+ **Frame slides:** Draws a pretty little black picture frame around each slide on the printout.

+ **Print hidden slides:** Includes images of hidden slides in your handouts, even if you don't show them in your slide show. This option is useful for providing audience participants with additional reference information that may be too elementary, too advanced, or too time-consuming to include in your formal presentation.

Printing Audience Handouts

Audiences appreciate copies of your slides — handouts make it easier for the audience to follow your presentation, plus they have a permanent record of what you said.

Audience handouts show miniatures of your slides, and if you want, you can include on each handout a header, a footer, and even lines where audience members can jot down notes.

The appearance of audience handouts depends on how many slides you want to cram onto a page — and subsequently how large you want each printed slide to appear. You have the option of printing two, three, four, six, or nine slides per page.

The three per page option offers a nice mix of adequate slide size and empty space for participants to jot down their own notes. But if you're an environmentally-conscious sort, go for the nine per page option and duplex your handouts front and back.

Print audience handouts as follows:

1. Choose File⇨Print from the Menu bar. The Print dialog box appears.

2. Select Handouts from the drop-down menu in the Print what area of the Print dialog box. This activates the Handouts area of the Print dialog box.

3. In the Handouts area, select the number of Slides per page you want from the drop-down menu. Your choices consist of 2, 3, 4, 6, or 9 slides per page.

4. If available, press the radio button indicating whether you want slides ordered Horizontal or Vertical. These radio buttons are available when you choose to print 4, 6, or 9 slides per page.

5. Click OK to start printing.

Printing Speaker Notes

Notes Pages can be printed for the PowerPoint presenter to use as speaker notes (his own little cheat sheet) as he clicks through a slide show. For more information about creating speaker notes, *see also* Part VI. To print your speaker notes, select Notes Pages in the Print <u>w</u>hat area of the Print dialog box; then click OK.

Printing Transparencies

If you choose to print transparencies, perform these steps prior to stuffing the little sheets of transparency plastic into your printer:

1. Choose <u>F</u>ile⇨Page Set<u>u</u>p from the Menu bar to open the Page Setup dialog box.

2. Choose Overhead from the <u>S</u>lides sized for drop-down.

3. In the Slides area, click the <u>P</u>ortrait option.

 If you're setting up an existing presentation for output as transparencies, you may need to examine how the previous list of steps affects each of your slides. You may need to move or resize slide elements to better fit them to the new vertical page orientation — particularly if you created your presentation for on-screen viewing in landscape orientation.

 While creating a presentation for display as transparencies, you should consider using a white background, limiting the use of elaborate graphics, and avoiding color unless you have access to a color printer. Also think about running a paper copy of your slides before you print them to transparency sheets — making an error on paper is much cheaper than making it on plastic!

 Be sure to check whether your printer has the capability of printing directly onto transparencies. Those that don't may melt or otherwise degrade while printing is in progress! Even if your printer is capable of printing transparencies, you need to make sure you pick transparency sheets that are designed for your type of printer. You also need to check which side of the transparency sheet is designated as the print surface. Printing on the wrong side of the sheet can result in poor image quality because the ink fails to properly bond with the plastic.

Printing 35mm Slides

PowerPoint slides can be printed for use in a 35mm slide carousel with a little extra effort. You need to ensure that your PowerPoint slide dimensions are sized for 35mm, and then you must take your final presentation to a special facility that churns out the little guys.

To set up your slides for 35mm printing, follow these steps:

1. Choose File➪Page Setup from the Menu bar to open the Page Setup dialog box.

2. Choose 35mm Slides from the Slides sized for drop-down menu.

3. In the Slides area click the Landscape option.

If you're setting up an existing presentation for output as 35mm slides, you may need to examine how the previous list of steps affects each of your slides. You may need to move or resize slide elements to better fit them to the new dimensions.

At your neighborhood photo lab

Take a disk file of your slide presentation to your local photo processing center. You may want to check whether they use Mac or Windows so you know how to format your disk.

Remember to embed True Type fonts so that your text prints out the same on the physical slides as it looks on-screen.

Because printing 35mm slides tends to be a bit pricey (around $10 per slide), you won't want to print too many. So avoid including animations, and for goodness sakes, avoid spelling errors!

Via Genigraphics

Genigraphics is a company that has a special arrangement with Microsoft and can create 35mm slides for you. All you have to do is send Genigraphics your presentation on disk or online. If you plan ahead you can get your slides for as cheap as $4.50 each for three-day turnaround. (But if you need a rush job, the slides cost you $13.50 each!) You can charge the work to a major credit card or have Genigraphics bill you. They even do large color posters, spiral-bound presentation booklets, and banners on the Goodyear blimp. Okay, so they won't do blimps.

The following steps show you how to use Genigraphics services:

1. Choose File➪Send To➪Genigraphics. This action starts the Genigraphics Wizard that leads you through the rest of the process.

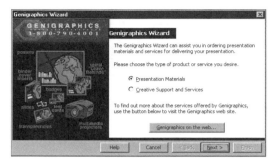

2. On the Genigraphics Wizard welcome screen, click <u>N</u>ext. Check the 35mm <u>s</u>lides output box or check another box that indicates your output preference.

3. Click <u>N</u>ext and select the presentation you want to send and how you want to send it. Genigraphics gives you the option of sending via modem, through the Internet, or on disk by snail mail.

4. Click <u>N</u>ext and continue to complete the questions the Wizard asks.

You need to decide on the type of slide mounts (plastic or glass), the shipping method, the ship-to location, the turn-around time (faster is more expensive), and the payment method.

Note: You need to complete two very important check boxes. One involves whether you want to print hidden slides — why would you? The other asks whether you want to print animation or not. With the exception of a slide that builds only the most critical point of your presentation, I wouldn't spend the money to print every animation of every slide. That's a quick way to turn a $4.50 slide into an $18 set of 4 slides — it's not worth it.

5. Continue clicking <u>N</u>ext until you have completed all the questions.

6. Click <u>F</u>inish. At this point, your modem delivers the order or you need to mail the disk.

Working through Microsoft Word

Instead of accessing and printing notes through individual Notes pages, you may prefer to compile and print your notes as a single Word document. You can also send audience handouts and outlines to Word for storage and printing as Word documents.

To send components of your PowerPoint presentation (notes, handouts, or an outline) to Microsoft Word, just follow these steps:

1. Choose File⇨Send To⇨Microsoft Word from the Menu bar. The Write-Up dialog box appears.

2. In the Page layout in Microsoft Word area, click the radio button indicating how you want to organize your Word document.

Choices consist of Notes next to slides, Blank lines next to slides, Notes below slides, Blank lines below slides, and Outline only.

3. In the Add slides to Microsoft Word document area, click the radio button indicating how you want slides added to your Microsoft Word document. Choices consist of

- **Paste:** Slide thumbnails are included in the Word document but remain unlinked with their source PowerPoint document. Changes in one document do not affect the other document.

- **Paste link:** Slide thumbnails are included in the Word document and are linked to their source PowerPoint document. Changes in either the Word or PowerPoint document are reflected in both documents.

4. Click OK to close the Write-Up dialog box.

Microsoft Word opens showing a new document that contains the components of the PowerPoint presentation that you selected. Choose File⇨Save from the Word Menu bar to save the Word document. Choose File⇨Print from the Word Menu bar to print the document.

Part IX

Using PowerPoint Online

You know how difficult it is to schedule a presentation or a meeting that fits everyone's schedule. You also know how frustrating it is when an absent colleague, customer, or student pesters you for a repeat performance of a presentation or lecture you delivered while they were out of the office (or vacationing in Bermuda). Well, stew no more. PowerPoint 2000 can alleviate your time-crunch angst with a smorgasbord of Web-based offerings for accommodating all audience members — even those with impossible schedules and geographic disadvantages.

In this part . . .

- ✔ **Navigating with hyperlinks**
- ✔ **Broadcasting a presentation on the Web**
- ✔ **Meeting online**
- ✔ **Publishing a presentation on the Web**
- ✔ **Conducting a threaded discussion on the Web**

Adding Hyperlinks

You can make text and clips into hyperlinks that can take you to just about anywhere — to another slide, another PowerPoint presentation, another program, or even a Web site. Clicking a hyperlink allows you to move directly to a specified location.

Follow these steps to add a hyperlink to a slide:

1. In Normal view or Slide view, select the text or clip that you want to designate as a hyperlink.

2. Choose Insert⇨Hyperlink from the Standard toolbar, press Ctrl+K, or click the Insert Hyperlink button on the Standard toolbar to bring up the Insert Hyperlink dialog box.

3. In the Text to display area, edit or accept the text that will serve as the hyperlink (if you chose an object, this option is deselected). If you edit the text in the dialog box, the text also changes on the slide.

4. Click the Screen Tip button to make the Set Hyperlink Screen Tip dialog box appear. Type the screen tip that you want to appear whenever the hyperlink is moused over.

5. In the Link to area on the left side of the dialog box, select the type of document the hyperlink will jump to. Options consist of

- **Existing File or Web Page:** Type the file or Web page name link in the designated box, or select from the lists of Recent Files, Browsed Pages, or Inserted Links presented in the dialog box. You can also click the Browse button and look for a File, Web Page, or Bookmark.

- **Place in This Document:** Choose a slide from the list in the area labeled Select a place in this document. The Slide preview area shows a thumbnail of your selected slide.

- **Create New Document:** Type a name in the Name of new document area and click Change to save the new document in a different folder than the one displayed. In the When to edit area, click the radio button indicating whether to Edit the new document later or Edit the new document now.

- **E-mail Address:** Complete the E-mail address and the Subject areas. Instead of typing the address, you may click a choice from the list of Recently used e-mail addresses.

6. Click OK to complete the creation of the hyperlink. Newly created text hyperlinks are highlighted in colors that coordinate with other text on your slide.

Hyperlinks become active only when you're running a slide show. So how can you be sure that you've created a hyperlink? Run the slide show to see whether the mouse pointer changes to a hand whenever it hovers over a hyperlink. If it does, the screen tip should appear, and a single click on the hyperlink should link you to the location you selected in the Insert Hyperlink dialog box.

To delete a hyperlink:

1. In Normal view or Slide view, click the hyperlink that you want to remove.

2. Click the Insert Hyperlink button on the Standard toolbar. This step may seem illogical, but it now brings up an Edit Hyperlink dialog box that appears with a heretofore-unseen button: Remove Link.

3. Click the Remove Link button and say "Hasta la Vista, baby" to your hyperlink.

Broadcasting a PowerPoint Presentation

PowerPoint 2000 offers the option of broadcasting your presentation over the Web. Broadcasting your presentation is ideal when you want to reach distant audiences that can't easily congregate in one physical place to view your show. Each audience participant needs only a computer, an Internet connection, and a Web browser to view the broadcast.

A Web broadcast works somewhat like a television broadcast: To view your show, people need the date, time, and "channel" where they can tune in. Microsoft Outlook or another e-mail program can be used to schedule the date and time of the Web broadcast. The channel is the URL (Uniform Resource Locator — the Web address) that participants must point their browsers to. You also have the option of archiving the broadcast on a Web server so that individuals who miss the show can access the presentation at a later time.

Setting up and scheduling a broadcast

PowerPoint assists you in scheduling a presentation for broadcast by working hand-in-hand with Microsoft Outlook. If you don't have Outlook installed, PowerPoint works instead with your e-mail program to send out messages inviting participants to view your future broadcast.

At the time of the broadcast, PowerPoint sends a broadcast-formatted version of your slide show to a server that you designate. Participants view the show by accessing the server.

As the presenter, you must use Microsoft Internet Explorer version 4.0 or later to conduct a Web broadcast.

To set up and schedule a currently open presentation for broadcast

1. Choose Slide Show➪Online Broadcast➪Set Up and Schedule from the Menu bar. (If you haven't saved your presentation, you see a warning dialog box informing you that the presentation must be saved before scheduling a broadcast.)

2. In the Broadcast Schedule dialog box that appears, choose one of three options for broadcasting your presentation:

- **Set up and schedule a new broadcast:** Choose this option and the Schedule a New Broadcast dialog box appears.

- **Change settings or reschedule a broadcast:** Available only if you have previously scheduled the current presentation for broadcast.

- **Replace a file that is currently scheduled for broadcast:** This command substitutes the current presentation for another that is already scheduled for broadcast. Use this option when you change or update the content of a presentation after it has already been scheduled.

For some really helpful tips on making your online broadcast a smashing success, click the Tips for Broadcast button in the Broadcast Schedule dialog box.

If you select Set up and schedule a new broadcast, the Schedule a New Broadcast dialog box appears.

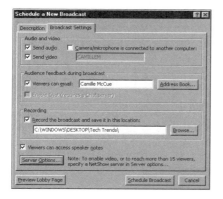

3. In the Schedule a New Broadcast dialog box, type in information for each of the following two tabs:

- **Description:** Type the information that you want to appear on the lobby page for the broadcast. Participants view the lobby page while waiting for the broadcast to start. Type a Title for the broadcast, a Description, a Speaker name, and a Contact name.

- **Broadcast Settings:** In the Audio and video area, click the check boxes to Send audio (if your presentation includes sounds) and Send video (if your presentation includes movies).

If you plan to broadcast video, you should do so from a fast computer (minimum 333 MHz) with a video card that performs hardware-based compression. You can also use a second computer to manage audio and video. To use video or audio from a computer other than your current system, click the check box for Camera/microphone is connected to another computer and type the name of that computer.

Note: Using live video with a camera requires that you broadcast via a NetShow server.

4. In the Audience feedback during broadcast area, click the Viewers can email check box if you want to enable viewers to e-mail questions and comments during the broadcast. Click the Address Book button to browse and select the e-mail delivery box. Click the Enable Chat check box if you want to give your viewers the ability to discuss your presentation in an online chat room. Using this feature requires that you have access to a Chat server.

5. In the Recording area, click the check box for Record the broadcast and save it in this location if you want to archive the broadcast for later use. Click the Browse button to select the location where you want the broadcast saved.

6. Click the check box for Viewers can access speaker notes if you want broadcast participants to see the notes pane section of your presentation.

7. Click the Server Options button. The Server Options dialog box appears.

8. In the Server Options dialog box, complete Step 1: (required) Specify a shared location. Click Browse to choose the folder where you want to place the presentation. This folder must be located on a server accessible to all audience participants.

If you want to use live video, you must use a local NetShow server to broadcast your presentation. Also, if you want to use prerecorded video with an audience of more than 15 participants, you must use a local NetShow server. If you want to reach audience members who are participating via the Internet, you must use a third party NetShow service provider. In any of these instances you must complete Step 2: (optional) Specify a NetShow server. For additional details on using this feature, click About NetShow Services where you will find online information. (Clicking About NetShow Services causes your computer to attempt to connect to the Internet.)

9. Click OK to close the Server Options dialog box.

10. Click the Schedule Broadcast button to schedule the broadcast and inform participants of its date, time, and URL. This starts your e-mail program. If you don't have Microsoft Outlook, type the date and time of the broadcast in the message. The message already includes the URL (online location) of the broadcast. Send the e-mail to participants you are inviting to the broadcast.

11. Click the Preview Lobby Page button to examine how the lobby page will appear. (Keep in mind that this lobby page is what invited participants will see as they patiently wait for your broadcast to commence.)

If you're using Outlook, the broadcast starts at your command, and you can schedule the presentation as you do any other meeting. If you or your recipients aren't using Outlook, the invitation mail has a hyperlink to the location of the broadcast.

It's a good idea to rehearse the broadcast. You can schedule the run-through with yourself as the only participant and go through all of the steps to make sure that everything is working properly.

Initiating a broadcast

Start your presentation broadcast as follows:

1. Approximately 30 minutes prior to your scheduled start time, open the PowerPoint presentation that you want to broadcast.

2. Choose Slide Show⇨Online Broadcast⇨Begin Broadcast from the Menu bar. PowerPoint saves your presentation (in HTML) for online broadcast from the server you previously selected in the Server Options dialog box. Pre-broadcast audio and video checks are performed as well.

3. (Optional) You can send a pre-broadcast message (for example, "The show will be delayed 5 minutes . . . I'm getting a cappuccino.") by clicking Audience Message. Type your message and click the Update button. The message is added to the lobby page where participants patiently wait for your show.

4. Begin the broadcast by clicking Start at the appointed time.

Viewing a broadcast

Prior to a broadcast, you receive an invitation announcing the date, time, and URL where you can view the scheduled PowerPoint slide show.

If you use Microsoft Outlook, you can accept the invitation so that your calendar reflects your participation in the broadcast. Accepting the invitation in Outlook also creates a reminder that appears on your computer 15 minutes prior to the start of the broadcast.

If you don't use Outlook, your invitation arrives as an e-mail message containing the broadcast information. Be sure to save the message.

You must have Microsoft Internet Explorer version 4.0 or later to take part in a PowerPoint broadcast.

To participate as an audience member in the broadcast, follow these steps about 10 minutes before the broadcast:

1. If you used Outlook to schedule your participation in the broadcast, open Outlook. If you received your broadcast invitation by e-mail, open that e-mail.

The first time you participate in a broadcast, you may be asked to download some ActiveX controls for Internet Explorer 4.0. Follow the downloading and installation instructions presented on-screen.

2. In Outlook, click the View Broadcast button on the broadcast reminder message. Non-Outlook users should click the URL listed for the broadcast.

Your browser window opens and displays the lobby page of the upcoming broadcast. The lobby page shows the presentation's title and description, along with the presenter's name and contact information. You also see any messages or reminders the presenter sends before starting the broadcast. A countdown signals the automatic start of the broadcast in your browser window.

3. View the presentation as it advances in your browser window. If the presenter has enabled certain features, you may be able to send e-mail questions during the broadcast. You may also be able to exchange comments with other audience members in a chat window.

If you join a presentation late, you can click View previous slides during the broadcast to view the slides that you missed.

Meeting Online

PowerPoint 2000 works hand in hand with Microsoft NetMeeting, allowing you to present a complete slide show that appears in real time on all participants' computers, right at their very own desks.

Online meetings differ dramatically from broadcasts in that participating colleagues can work collaboratively, providing input and making changes to the presentation as the meeting proceeds. ***See also*** "Broadcasting a PowerPoint Presentation" earlier in this part for more information on broadcasts.

All participants in an online meeting must have PowerPoint 2000 and NetMeeting installed on their computers.

Setting up an online meeting

If you use Microsoft Outlook, schedule an online meeting using these steps:

1. In PowerPoint, open the presentation that you want to discuss.

2. Choose Tools⇨Online Collaboration⇨Schedule Meeting from the Menu bar, and the Microsoft NetMeeting dialog box appears.

3. Fill in the information in the Microsoft NetMeeting dialog box. This dialog box appears only the first time you use NetMeeting. Click OK. Microsoft Outlook starts and opens a new meeting form.

4. Complete the Outlook form to schedule the meeting and invite selected colleagues to the meeting. (Consult the Help menus in Outlook for additional information.)

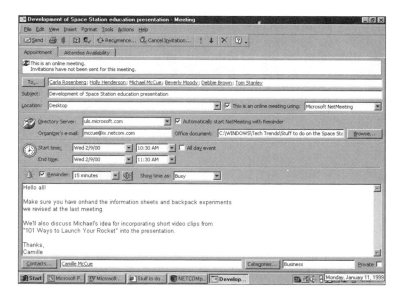

To initiate an unplanned meeting, follow these steps:

1. In PowerPoint, open the presentation that you want to discuss.

2. Choose <u>T</u>ools⇨<u>O</u>nline Collaboration⇨<u>M</u>eet Now from the Menu bar. The Place A Call dialog box appears.

Note: If the Microsoft NetMeeting dialog box appears, fill in the requested information. This dialog box only appears the first time you use NetMeeting.

3. Select the names of the persons you want to invite to the online meeting and click <u>C</u>all after each name. If a person you want to invite is not listed, choose another directory in the Directory box. (NetMeeting sets up an account for you in the Directory the first time you run the program.)

To receive an invitation to join an unplanned online meeting, each invitee must be running Microsoft NetMeeting on his or her computer.

Your online meeting begins when one or more persons accepts your invitation.

Joining an online meeting

If you're scheduled, in Outlook, to host or simply participate in an online meeting, you receive an online meeting reminder in advance of the meeting. If you aren't an Outlook user, keep the e-mail invitation you send or receive as a reminder of the meeting's scheduled date and time.

   ✦ To join the meeting, click Join this NetMeeting.

   ✦ To decline the invitation to meet, click Dismiss this reminder.

When the meeting is scheduled to begin, you receive an online meeting call, and a Join Meeting dialog box appears on your screen. (*Note:* You must have NetMeeting open on your computer to join the meeting.)

✦ To join the meeting, click Accept. Accepting the invitation causes the shared presentation to appear on your computer screen.

✦ To decline the invitation to meet, click Ignore.

Hosting a slide show during the meeting

As meeting host, you can relinquish control of the presentation to meeting participants so that they can edit your presentation:

✦ To allow participants to edit the presentation during the meeting, click the Allow others to edit button on the Online Meeting toolbar. The initials of the person currently controlling the presentation are then attached to the mouse pointer. When this collaboration feature is enabled, each participant in the meeting can take turns editing and controlling the presentation.

✦ As host, you can regain control of the presentation during collaboration by pressing the Esc key and clicking to deselect the Allow others to edit button. Participants can continue working collaboratively via the Chat Window and the Whiteboard.

You can call new participants and invite them to join the meeting, you can remove participants, and you can end the meeting. All participants can engage in an online discussion via the Chat Window. Participants can also post and edit notes, slides, figures, and other documents via the Whiteboard. You can access all of these functions through the Online Meeting toolbar that appears whenever you are engaged in a NetMeeting.

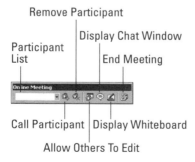

Participating collaboratively in the meeting

At any time during the meeting, the host can turn over editing control of the presentation to meeting participants. Only one person (whether it's the host or a participant) can edit the presentation at a time. To obtain control and edit the shared presentation for the first time, use your mouse to double-click anywhere in the presentation. Then use standard PowerPoint editing procedures to make changes to the presentations. After you make your first edits, regain control by clicking anywhere in the presentation.

The host can remove editing control from participants whenever he wants. When you're not in control of the presentation, you may instead find it useful to collaborate with other meeting participants through the Chat Window or Whiteboard.

Working in the Chat Window

The Chat Window offers online meeting participants a structured area for exchanging comments. During the meeting, both the host and the participants can type in the Chat Window and can see comments typed by fellow meeting participants. Each message is labeled with the name of the message sender so that participants can keep track of who says what.

The host of the online meeting opens the Chat Window for use by meeting participants. If you're hosting an online meeting, get the chat under way by following these steps:

1. Click the Display Chat Window button in the Online Meeting toolbar.

2. Whenever you wish to send a message, type in the Message area and press Enter.

3. After the Chat Window is open, participants can send their own messages by typing in the Message area and pressing Enter. The running conversation scrolls from top to bottom in the window.

Working on the Whiteboard

The Whiteboard provides the online meeting host and participants with a combination clipboard/drawing area. This area can be used for pasting images, doodling drawings, and sharing visual ideas among meeting participants.

The host of the online meeting opens the Whiteboard for use by meeting participants. When you're hosting an online meeting, open the Whiteboard as follows:

1. Click the Display Whiteboard button in the Online Meeting toolbar.

2. Click the Whiteboard and use the drawing tools and menu functions to create drawings, type text, and paste images.

3. After the Whiteboard is open, participants can add their own images and doodles by clicking the Whiteboard window.

Ending an online meeting

The host is the only person who can end the online meeting for all participants, although individual participants can choose to duck out at any time (much like a regular face-to-face meeting!):

+ **To end a meeting in which you are the host:** Click the End Meeting button on the Online Meeting toolbar.

+ **To disconnect from a meeting in which you are a participant:** Click the End Meeting button on the Online Meeting toolbar.

When the meeting is over, the host can choose to save changes made to the PowerPoint presentation during the meeting. The host can also choose to save the text in the Chat Window by choosing File⇨Save from the Chat Menu bar. The host can save the contents of the Whiteboard by choosing File⇨Save from the Whiteboard Menu bar.

Publishing on the Web

You can give your presentation some longevity and added accessibility by posting it on the Web. Thanks to PowerPoint, you don't need to know how to write HTML code to publish your show online. PowerPoint 2000 offers a quick and easy option for translating your slide shows into the HTML language required for publishing Web pages online.

Saving a presentation as a Web page

To post your PowerPoint presentation to the Web, you must save the file in HTML format — the language of the Web. Saving your presentation in HTML makes it possible to display and view your presentation in a Web browser such as Netscape or Internet Explorer. Saving your slide show as a Web page also sets the Web page title and the location where the file is stored.

The following saving procedure doesn't automatically make your presentation available for viewing online. You have to save it on a Web server for other people to have access to it. *See also* "Placing a presentation on a Web server" later in this part for more information.

To save your presentation as a Web page:

1. Choose File⇨Save as Web Page from the Menu bar. The Save As dialog box appears. Any other PowerPoint presentations you save as Web pages are listed here. You may have to browse to see the other presentations that you have saved.

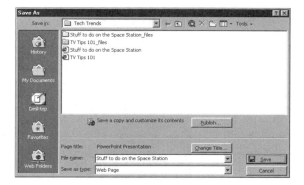

2. In the Save As dialog box, click the Publish button. The Publish as Web Page dialog box appears.

3. In the Publish as Web Page dialog box, you can make adjustments to the following attributes that affect how your presentation is saved:

- **Publish what?:** Choices consist of the Complete presentation; a specific range of slides selected by typing in start and end slides in the Slide number area; or a Custom show selected from the drop-down menu. You can also click the Display speaker notes check box to include speaker notes on the Web page.

  Clicking Web Options summons a Web Options dialog box where you can make additional choices about how your presentation is shown in the Web browser, and how users navigate the presentation. The Web Options dialog box has four tabs: General, Files, Pictures, and Encoding. The

General tab provides choices regarding the appearance of your presentation in the browser window, including the choice of adding navigation controls (and how those controls look); the option of playing or disabling animation; and the option of resizing graphics to fit the browser window. The Files tab provides options for naming and locating the Web files. The Pictures tab offers choices of picture file formats. Encoding offers a large selection of options for the browser language in which the presentation is saved.

- **Browser support:** Choose which browsers the presentation will be displayed on. Choosing Microsoft Internet Explorer version 4.0 or later (high fidelity) ensures that users are able to take advantage of advanced Web browser features like animations, sounds, and movies. Choosing Microsoft Internet Explorer or Netscape Navigator version 3.0 or later expands your accessible audience by allowing users with older browsers to view your presentation — although they aren't able to experience the bells and whistles that are present with a more advanced browser. Choosing the All browsers listed above option creates larger files but allows for virtually anyone with any kind of browser (including WebTV users) to access your presentation.

- **Publish a copy as:** Accept the current page title or click the Change button to summon the Set Page Title dialog box and type in the name of your presentation for the browser title bar. Also type a name for your presentation in the File name area, or click Browse to change the location where you want your resulting Web files stored.

- **Open published Web page in browser:** Click this check box to view your presentation as a Web page upon saving it.

4. Click Publish to accept your choices and save your presentation.

Saving your file as a Web page organizes all the components of your presentation (like text, graphics, and sound) into a special Web folder. The default name of this folder is the name of the presentation file followed by the word "files."

The very first time you save a presentation as a Web page, PowerPoint converts all the graphic images in the presentation to one of three Web-supported formats: GIF, JPEG, or PNG. The more graphics you include in your presentation, the more time this initial save takes.

Placing a presentation on a Web server

If you want to make your PowerPoint presentations available
online, you need access to a Web server where you can save your
presentations. Placing a presentation on a Web server can also
make it available to colleagues on your company intranet.

To create a Web folder where you can save Web page files on a
Web server, do the following:

✦ **To create a new Web folder while you're working in
   PowerPoint:** Choose File➪Open from the Menu bar and click
   Web Folders on the Places Bar in the Open dialog box. Click
   the Create New Folder button and type in the information
   requested by the Add Web Folder Wizard.

✦ **For a URL already on a Web server:** Choose File➪Save As to
   summon the Save As dialog box. Type a Web address (such as
   `http://Camilleserver/public/`) in the File name box
   and click Save to create a Web folder at that location on the
   Web. You must have the appropriate access rights to create
   the folder on the Web server.

Previewing a presentation as a Web page

To view a saved Web page presentation in a Web browser, choose
File➪Web page preview from the Menu bar. Your default Web
browser opens and displays the PowerPoint presentation using
the attributes you set in the Web Options dialog box.

You can now navigate the presentation just as you do any Web
document. You can scroll forward and backward through your
slides, and you can jump to a particular slide by clicking that slide
in the outline pane on the left side of the screen.

Test-driving your Web page presentation this way gives you a good look at how other people will view your presentation in their browser windows.

Using Threaded Discussions for Collaboration

PowerPoint 2000 allows you — and anyone viewing your slide show — to post annotated comments online with the presentation. The Discussions feature is only available with Microsoft Office Server Extensions. Your computer system administrator must install and set up this feature.

Discussion comments are threaded, meaning that multiple discussions can be posted for each presentation, with each discussion consisting of related comments. An individual viewing your presentation on the Web can post a remark to any discussion, and you (and others) can respond to that remark. The discussions don't have to occur in real time. Remarks can be posted, read, and responded to at the convenience of each person. Follow these steps to start a discussion about a PowerPoint presentation on the Web:

1. In your Web browser, open the presentation that you want to discuss.

2. Choose Tools⇨Online Collaboration⇨Web Discussions from the Menu bar.

3. On the Discussions toolbar, choose Discussions⇨Insert about the Presentation. The discussion pane appears.

4. Type the subject of the discussion in the Discussion subject area; then type your comment in Discussion text.

5. Click OK to add your comment to the discussion.

Part X

Tips, Tricks, and Troubleshooting

Consider this part your PowerPoint five-and-dime store. Here you can find advice about managing hordes of slide show files and speeding up your work with keystroke shortcuts — advice a good PowerPoint user like yourself is wise to follow. And for the nerd that dwells deep within you . . . well, that nerd will be especially thrilled with this part's answers to your programming questions regarding macros and virus-checking.

Most importantly, this part covers therapeutic ways of dealing with Murphy's Law disasters, which inevitably plague even the most innocuous PowerPoint user. You find out how to troubleshoot every difficulty from printing to projection — and fix those pesky problems like a real PowerPoint pro.

In this part . . .

- ✔ **Recording and using macros**
- ✔ **Managing PowerPoint files**
- ✔ **Troubleshooting presentation problems**
- ✔ **Moving around quickly with keystroke shortcuts**

Automating Tasks with Macros

A *macro* is a user-customized shortcut, an opportunity to develop your own time-saving tricks to employ when creating your presentation.

For example, I always start each new PowerPoint file by opening the Slide Master and changing all my fonts to 32-point bold Arial. To accomplish this task without a macro, I have to go through five different steps. It's a real hassle. But by recording a macro, I can generate a single menu option that performs the entire sequence of steps.

To create a macro, you perform a series of keystrokes and menu selections and then give your creation a one-touch name. This process is known as *recording a macro.*

While recording a macro, you can use the mouse and mouse buttons for clicking toolbar button commands and choosing menu options — but not for recording mouse movements in a presentation window. For example, you can't record mouse movements such as selecting text, dragging clip art to a new location, or clicking all slide objects to create a group. Mouse movements in the presentation window must instead be performed with the toolbar, menu, or keyboard; for example, to record a macro for selecting all slide objects, you must choose Edit⇨Select All from the Menu bar.

Recording a macro

Follow these steps to record a macro for a procedure:

1. Perform a dry run of the sequence you plan to record as a macro.

2. Choose Tools⇨Macro⇨Record New Macro. The Record Macro dialog box appears with three empty boxes for you to complete: Macro name, Store macro in, and Description.

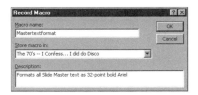

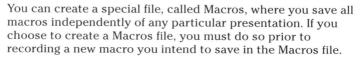

3. In the Macro name area, type a name for the macro. The name can't contain spaces, commas, or periods. If you don't type a name, PowerPoint gives the macro a default name such as Macro1. ·

4. In the Store macro in area, choose a presentation where you want to store the macro. The default storage location is the current presentation.

 You can create a special file, called Macros, where you save all macros independently of any particular presentation. If you choose to create a Macros file, you must do so prior to recording a new macro you intend to save in the Macros file.

5. (Optional) Type a Description of the macro, indicating what actions it performs. If you don't type a description, a default phrase appears indicating who recorded the macro and when it was recorded.

6. Click OK. The Record Macro dialog box closes, and the Stop Recording box appears in its place.

7. Perform the keystroke and menu sequence that you want the macro to record. Don't worry if you make a mistake — just stop, return to Step 1, and record again.

8. When you finish recording, click the Stop button.

The macro is now recorded and is named whatever you called it in the Record Macro dialog box.

Running a macro

Follow these steps to run a macro:

1. Choose Tools⇨Macro⇨Macros.

The Macro dialog box opens and lists all available macros you have recorded. The Macro in area lets you switch to other PowerPoint presentations so that you can use macros you recorded in those files.

2. Click the macro you want to run.

3. Click Run.

Editing a macro

Editing a macro is a relatively complex task — one that requires you to trudge through lines of code created in a programming language called Visual Basic.

Unless you're a glutton for punishment (and you actually enjoy tinkering with computer code), your bet best for editing a macro is to delete the macro and record it again from scratch.

Protecting against macro viruses

Like all other computer files, your PowerPoint presentations are susceptible to computer viruses — nasty "infections" you'll want to take measures to guard against. PowerPoint presentations typically come into contact with a specific type of virus — a macro virus — which resides in a macro of a presentation or a design template.

PowerPoint itself doesn't offer anti-virus protection in that it can't hunt down and eliminate existing file-damaging viruses on your system. But it can provide extra levels of security to help reduce potential infection of your files by viruses transmitted when you open macros created by other persons.

To select a level of security when using macros created by other people, open the Security dialog box by choosing Tools⇨Macros⇨ Security from the Menu bar.

On the Security Level tab, choose from High, Medium, or Low levels of protection when enabling macros transmitted by outside sources:

✦ Selecting High allows only macros from trusted sources to run. Macros from all other sources are automatically disabled.

✦ Selecting Medium causes you to be notified whenever an outside macro is attempting to be used on your system. You have the option of accepting or rejecting the macro for each notification.

✦ Selecting Low enables all macros to be used on your system, regardless of the source. It's probably not safe to choose this option unless you already have virus-detection software installed on your computer.

On the Trusted Sources tab, you can list names of persons whom you know to be safe sources. Macros transmitted by these trusted sources are automatically enabled.

Managing Your PowerPoint Files

As a teacher, I'm an inherent pack rat: I save every paper, widget, videotape, and newspaper clipping I may someday want to use to teach a concept. If only I could remember which of my 30-odd boxes I actually stuffed that one particular widget in . . . or if it's really in a box at all.

After working with PowerPoint a while, you may find it hard to locate that one particular PowerPoint widget you need. I strongly recommend organizing and cataloging your PowerPoint projects so that locating and retrieving presentations is a fruitful process. Here are some tips on how to manage PowerPoint files to your best advantage.

Naming and grouping files logically

Maintain consistency in naming files so that you can easily distinguish the contents of one presentation from another without wasting time opening the file. Use a fairly long name that includes the date and ends with PPT as the filename extension (for example, BusExpoAug99.PPT). For files you plan to store on the Internet, avoid using spaces and symbols in the name.

I find that using folders to logically group like topics together is helpful. You may wish to group by date (months or quarterly cycles) or by subject matter. Keep call-to files (like movies) in the same folder with the presentation that calls them.

Whatever you do, don't store your PowerPoint presentations in the PowerPoint program folder — keep your presentations in their own special location, separate from the program files. Keeping your presentations in a specially named folder makes it easier to backup that folder onto other media (such as a Zip disk) on a regular basis. If you keep your presentations in the same folder as PowerPoint's program files, it's difficult to sort through which items are which.

Backing up your work

Most people don't realize the necessity of backing up their work until they experience the agony of losing irreplaceable computer files. Trust me, nothing is worse than working for hours (or days!) to develop a PowerPoint slide show extravaganza, only to have it vanish forever during a freak system failure. Consider backing up your files like buying insurance: Nobody's happy about doing it until tragedy strikes.

The method of backup you choose is entirely up to you. If you have only a handful of critical files, copying everything to a 100MB Zip disk will suffice. But if you have loads and loads of data, you may need to write your files to a recordable CD-ROM or a 1GB (or 2GB) Jaz disk. You can also use Microsoft Backup, a program that performs incremental backup of only the files that have changed that day. Don't feel compelled to rush out and buy Microsoft Backup — you probably already have it because it's a component of Windows 95 and Windows 98. Look for it under Start➪Programs➪Accessories➪System Tools.

You should also back up any files you plan to transport between your home and your office or any other place you plan to access your computer files. When you shuttle files via a notebook computer, consider also making a floppy copy of files — and carrying the floppy separate from the notebook in a nonmagnetic case. If you're really paranoid about losing stuff, you can also send your file as an e-mail attachment from your office account to your home account and vice versa.

Recording document properties

Recording document properties allows you to jot down and keep notes to yourself — and others — regarding the purpose and content of a PowerPoint presentation. This isn't a really high-profile feature of PowerPoint, but it is useful for labeling files for future reference, particularly when you deal with lots and lots of presentations.

A PowerPoint document's properties include its filename and directory, the template used to create the file, and other information you provide, such as the presentation's title, subject, author, keywords, and comments.

To examine or update a document's properties

1. Open the file.

2. Choose <u>F</u>ile➪Proper<u>t</u>ies from the Menu bar. A Properties dialog box appears.

3. Click the Summary tab to add/update file properties.

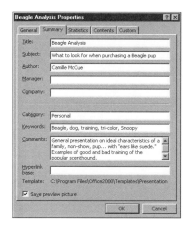

4. Click OK.

5. Choose <u>F</u>ile➪<u>S</u>ave to save changes.

Troubleshooting

Although you probably don't plan on your house burning down any day in the near future, you likely have taken out fire insurance nonetheless. With this same thinking in mind, you should create your own insurance for computer troubleshooting for the future. That way, when you are in crunch time, you have the knowledge to get through the crisis.

Automatically repairing PowerPoint

PowerPoint, and each of the Office 2000 programs, offers a feature which finds and fixes problems associated with all Office programs installed on your system. This feature, called Detect and Repair, can help with system problems like missing files and corrupted registry settings, but it can't help repair personal documents created by the Office applications themselves.

To automatically detect and repair problem PowerPoint files, follow these steps:

1. Choose Help⇨Detect and Repair from the Menu bar. The Detect and Repair dialog box appears.

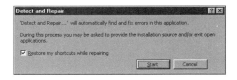

2. (Optional) Click the Restore my shortcuts while repairing check box to restore program shortcuts to the Windows Start menu.

3. Click Start.

If Detect and Repair fails to fix PowerPoint, consider reinstalling the program altogether.

Locating a file

Choosing File⇨Open allows you to access search criteria that can help you retrieve files:

✦ **File name:** Lets you specify any portion of the filename your brain may selectively recall.

✦ **Files of type:** Allows you to specify the file type for which you are searching. This is a great option when, for example, you know that the file you seek is a Word document or an Excel spreadsheet.

In the Open dialog box, you can also click the arrow beside <u>T</u>ools and select <u>F</u>ind to open a Find dialog box with extensive options for locating files.

Selecting a slide object

One of the most annoying and commonplace PowerPoint frustrations occurs when you try to click a slide object — like a text box or a clip art — and you find that you can't select it, no matter what. Somewhere between scratching your head and throwing your computer against the wall, you realize the simple truth: the object resides on the Slide Master. Switch to Slide Master view and try to select the object again.

Speeding up a slow presentation

If your slide graphics are very elaborate, you may find that an eternity passes between when you click the mouse and when you transition to the next slide. Try reformatting slide graphics in an editing program by reducing the number of colors or saving graphics images in a more compressed format to reduce file size. Move repeatedly used images in a presentation from individual slides to the Slide Master. Consider copying and running your presentation from your computer's hard drive to decrease access time. Performing a complete dry run of a slide show before actually conducting the presentation in front of an audience also helps.

Finding a lost movie

Another common slide show problem involves forgetting to bundle movies along with your presentation. Remember, movies are not merged with other PowerPoint elements like text and graphics — they remain as stand-alone files which play on command during the slide show. If you copy your PowerPoint presentation to another computer, you must copy the movie files along with the presentation.

Saving your work in an organized manner makes finding lost movies much easier. Consistent file organization also makes it less likely you'll lose your files in the first place! *See* "Managing Your PowerPoint Files" earlier in this part for guidance in organizing all related files into one folder.

Solving equipment problems

If you plan on presenting a sound-enhanced slide show, check that the system on which you'll be showing your show has sound capabilities. Make sure that speakers are properly connected and that they play loud enough for larger audiences to clearly hear your embedded audio.

Consider what level of display power you require to present to your intended audiences. Taking along an LCD panel with your notebook requires only that your presentation location provide an overhead projector — but LCD panels tend to be somewhat pricey and have poor color contrast. If you use one, make certain that you use high contrast colors between text and background — and kill the use of small clip art or detailed photographic images.

A scan converter that connects your notebook to a television may be the best compromise of cheap and professional, but be warned: I implore you to check that the TV you'll be borrowing sports the necessary connections for mating with your converter. I've been caught often with a TV that has every plug except the one I need to connect my scan converter. You may need to route the scan converter through the RCA video-in jack on a VCR, then connect the VCR to the TV using an RCA-to-coaxial cable. A VHS player will not suffice, because it doesn't have a video-in jack — only a video-out jack. A little research can save you a lot of headaches.

It also behooves you to take along your own cables, including extension cords and surge protectors. They're cheap and transportable, and their ready presence will make you feel better. You never know what you just might have to plug into at the other end.

And for the really paranoid among you, take along a set of overhead transparencies of your presentation as a backup. There's nothing like peace of mind!

Solving printing problems

In the event that your PowerPoint presentation poops out your printer, try investigating the following rundown of potential offenders:

✦ Check that the printer's power cord is plugged in and that the printer is turned on.

✦ Check the printer cable to ensure that it's connected to the printer port on your computer if you're using a serial or parallel connection.

✦ Check that the printer itself is set to Operate or is in online mode.

✦ If you print to a network printer, examine the printer queue to ensure that no one is tying up the printer ahead of you.

✦ Check to make sure there's plenty of paper in the printer tray and that the ink cartridge is functioning.

✦ Make sure the printer is available and listed in the Printer Name area of the Print dialog box. *See* Part VIII for details on working with the Print dialog box.

Using Keyboard Shortcuts

For tasks you perform repeatedly, several snappy shortcuts are available. Consider committing a handful of your most frequently used tasks to memory — shortcuts can save you a tremendous amount of time in the long run.

Text shortcuts

The following table tells you about keyboard shortcuts that replace menu and toolbar commands you use to edit slide text.

Press This	To Change Highlighted Text to This
Ctrl+B	**Bold**
Ctrl+I	*Italic*
Ctrl+U	Underline
Ctrl+spacebar	Remove all formatting
Ctrl+E	Centered text
Ctrl+L	Left-aligned text
Ctrl+R	Right-aligned text
Ctrl+J	Justified text
Ctrl+X	Cuts highlighted text
Ctrl+C	Copies highlighted text
Ctrl+V	Pastes highlighted text
Ctrl+A	Selects all text

Slide Master shortcuts

The following table shows you shortcuts that replace menu commands you use to summon Masters.

Press This	To Call Up This Master
Shift+Slide View button	Slide Master or Title Master
Shift+Outline View button	Handout Master
Shift+Slide Sorter View button	Handout Master

Other common shortcuts

Try these keyboard shortcuts to replace menu and toolbar commands you use to perform common tasks.

Press This	To Perform This Function
Ctrl+X	Cuts a selected object
Ctrl+C	Copies a selected object
Ctrl+V	Pastes a selected object
Ctrl+A	Selects all objects
Ctrl+N	Creates a new document
Ctrl+O	Opens an existing document
Ctrl+S	Saves your work
Ctrl+P	Prints your presentation
Ctrl+M	Creates a new slide

Index

Dummies Books™
Bestsellers on Every Topic!

Dummies Books™
Bestsellers on Every Topic!

WWW.DUMMIES.COM

Discover Dummies™ Online!

The Dummies Web Site is your fun and friendly online resource for the latest information about ...For Dummies® books on all your favorite topics. From cars to computers, wine to Windows, and investing to the Internet, we've got a shelf full of ...For Dummies books waiting for you!

Ten Fun and Useful Things You Can Do at www.dummies.com

1. Register this book and win!
2. Find and buy the ...For Dummies books you want online.
3. Get ten great Dummies Tips™ every week.
4. Chat with your favorite ...For Dummies authors.
5. Subscribe free to The Dummies Dispatch™ newsletter.
6. Enter our sweepstakes and win cool stuff.
7. Send a free cartoon postcard to a friend.
8. Download free software.
9. Sample a book before you buy.
10. Talk to us. Make comments, ask questions, and get answers!

Jump online to these ten fun and useful things at

http://www.dummies.com/10useful

For other technology titles from IDG Books Worldwide, go to
www.idgbooks.com

Not online yet? It's easy to get started with *The Internet For Dummies*, 5th Edition, or *Dummies 101®: The Internet For Windows® 98*, available at local retailers everywhere.

Find other ...*For Dummies* books on these topics:
Business • Careers • Databases • Food & Beverages • Games • Gardening • Graphics
Hardware • Health & Fitness • Internet and the World Wide Web • Networking • Office Suites
Operating Systems • Personal Finance • Pets • Programming • Recreation • Sports
Spreadsheets • Teacher Resources • Test Prep • Word Processing

IDG BOOKS WORLDWIDE BOOK REGISTRATION

Register This Book and Win!

We want to hear from you!

Visit **http://my2cents.dummies.com** to register this book and tell us how you liked it!

- Get entered in our monthly prize giveaway.

- Give us feedback about this book — tell us what you like best, what you like least, or maybe what you'd like to ask the author and us to change!

- Let us know any other *...For Dummies*® topics that interest you.

Your feedback helps us determine what books to publish, tells us what coverage to add as we revise our books, and lets us know whether we're meeting your needs as a *...For Dummies* reader. You're our most valuable resource, and what you have to say is important to us!

Not on the Web yet? It's easy to get started with *Dummies 101*®*: The Internet For Windows*® *98* or *The Internet For Dummies*,® 5th Edition, at local retailers everywhere.

Or let us know what you think by sending us a letter at the following address:

...For Dummies Book Registration
Dummies Press
7260 Shadeland Station, Suite 100
Indianapolis, IN 46256-3917
Fax 317-596-5498

BESTSELLING
BOOK SERIES